Special
Business Interests
and the
Open Door Policy

BY

CHARLES S. CAMPBELL, JR.

ARCHON BOOKS
1968

Library of Congress Catalog Card Number: 68-21689
Printed in the United States of America

PREFACE

Relations with China have for long been of the utmost importance to the United States. According to the Department of State's publication, *United States Relations with China*, released in August, 1949, American policy toward that country "has been based on the twin principles of (1) equality of commercial opportunity, and (2) the maintenance of the territorial and administrative integrity and political independence of China." [1] Some fifty years ago in notes sent to six of the great powers from September to November, 1899, the United States announced its support of the first of these principles, and in a circular dated July 3, 1900, its support of the second. Together the two principles constitute the essential features of the Open Door Policy.[2]

This book examines the part played by certain American business interests in bringing the government to adopt the principles put forward in the two sets of notes. It does not attempt to provide a complete explanation of the origins of the Open Door Policy. Of the several influences upon the government it considers only one. Satisfactory accounts already exist of most of these influences, whereas no one has dealt at any length with business pressure. The present study seeks to fill the gap and thereby to throw further light on the adoption of a policy which has been of tremendous import to the United States.

I wish to express my gratitude for generous assistance, not only in the preparation of this book but in a great number of other matters as well, to Professor Samuel Flagg Bemis, in whose seminar at Yale University I began my investigation of the Open Door Policy.

1. Department of State, *United States Relations with China, with Special Reference to the Period 1944–1949* (U. S. Government Printing Office, August, 1949), p. 1.
2. People sometimes explain the phrase "Open Door Policy" by reference to the first principle only, that is, "equality of commercial opportunity." But it appears preferable, when speaking in the context of American relations with China, to define the policy as including the second principle as well.

CONTENTS

	Preface	v
I	The Bogey of the Surplus	1
II	The Potential Market	10
III	The Actual Market	19
IV	Organization of a Propaganda	25
V	The Campaign Under Way	32
VI	Wartime Interlude	38
VII	Crisis	45
VIII	The September Notes	53
IX	Further Pressure	59
X	The July Circular	67
	Appendix	75
	Bibliographical Note	79
	Index	85

I

THE BOGEY OF THE SURPLUS

A FREQUENTLY expressed belief in American business circles in the late 1890's was that the Chinese Empire would some day become a tremendously valuable market. So widespread did this idea come to be that it created a climate of opinion favorable to the adoption of the Open Door Policy by the pro-business administration of President McKinley. Whence came this preoccupation with China? Part of the answer lies in a particular interpretation of American economic conditions which was prevalent among businessmen.

It was accepted doctrine with many businessmen—and with many in other fields too—that as a consequence of the tremendous growth of industry since the Civil War the United States was suffering from overproduction.[1] The domestic market was thought to be "saturated," weighed down by a mountainous "surplus" which could not be consumed at home and which, as time went on, would inevitably become greater and greater. New inventions and improved machinery would so increase productive capacity above possibilities of consumption that factories would be able to operate with profit barely half the year. This gloomy picture, held up to the Connecticut State Board of Trade in 1898,[2] had considerable vogue among businessmen.

The trend of United States foreign commerce seemed to substantiate such a dark prospect.[3] Between 1893 and 1898 the

1. See a series of three articles on the American "dilemma of having a productive capacity far in excess of ability to consume." *Journal of Commerce and Commercial Bulletin,* May 25, 26, and 27, 1897.

2. *Proceedings of the Connecticut State Board of Trade, 1891–1906* (New Haven, 1908), Ninth Annual Meeting, October 19, 1898, p. 24.

3. *Foreign Trade of the United States, 1893–98*
(in dollars)

Year Ending June 30	Imports	Exports	Debit Balance (−) Credit Balance (+)
1893	866,400,922	847,665,194	− 18,735,728
1894	654,994,622	892,140,572	+ 237,145,950
1895	731,969,965	807,538,165	+ 75,568,200

balance of trade shifted from a slight excess of imports to well over a half billion dollars of excess exports—an enormous reversal which to some appeared not only awe-inspiring but alarming. For although the change reflected an amazing growth in production, to many it indicated altogether too rapid growth as well as a home market alarmingly saturated. A profound transformation in the economic relationship of the United States with the rest of the world seemed to have overtaken an unsuspecting country. Here was ground for sober consideration. Such a radical transformation required an equally radical change in policy. In particular it appeared to point to the urgency of an all-out drive for overseas markets, because unless the country succeeded in adding substantially to its outlets abroad it would in time be swamped with an ever-growing surplus; the standard of living would decline; the social order would be disturbed; even revolution might break out —such was the firm conviction of many.

This alarmist point of view pervaded the business press in the late 1890's. "Let the foreign outlets for . . . surplus products be closed, and no protective policy can save the American manufacturer and laborer from the destructive effects of over-production," said the *Journal of Commerce*.[4] *Bradstreet's* in 1898 found manufacturers paying "almost single devotion" [5] to exporting their goods; and a year later the president of the National Association of Manufacturers reported that during the preceding three years the activities of the association had been "devoted mainly in the promotion of the foreign trade of our members." [6] In its editorials the *Iron Age* grew increasingly insistent on the importance of the export trade. Addressing the Manufacturers' Association of Illinois, a speaker emphasized the need of the United States, because of overproduction, to widen outlets "in every possible way." [7] "Competition in most lines of industry," declared the *United States Investor*, "has reached the point where an outlet for surplus stocks

1896	779,724,674	882,606,938	+ 102,882,264
1897	764,730,412	1,050,993,556	+ 286,263,144
1898	616,049,654	1,231,482,330	+ 615,432,676

The figures are from *Annual Review of the Foreign Commerce of the United States and Summary Tables of Commerce for the Year Ending June 30, 1911* (Washington, 1912), p. 44.

4. *Journal of Commerce and Commercial Bulletin*, February 1, 1899.

5. *Bradstreet's, 26* (1898), 66.

6. *Journal of Commerce and Commercial Bulletin*, January 26, 1899.

7. *Ibid.*, June 26, 1899.

becomes an imperative necessity." [8] Indeed, according to an authoritative scholar the conviction of the future dependence of American industry upon foreign markets was "almost universal." [9]

Numerous associations and clubs engaged in export promotion testified to belief in such dependence. Prominent among them was the Philadelphia Commercial Museum. For the benefit of exporters this institution maintained an exhibit of natural and manufactured products coming from all parts of the world, kept on file about a thousand trade journals in many languages, and supported special agents in countries of interest to American businessmen. [10] Congress in 1898 demonstrated its esteem for the museum by appropriating $350,000 for enlarging and making permanent the exhibit in Philadelphia. [11]

A further indication of the emphasis on exporting appeared in the contemporary movement for reform of the consular service. [12] Proposals for reform figured prominently in the business press and in a great majority of the periodic reports issued by major concerns, usually with stress on the relationship between well-trained consuls and export promotion. [13] Several business organizations, the most active of which were the New York and Cleveland Chambers of Commerce and the Merchants' Association of New York, devoted themselves to propaganda for a better consular service. [14]

8. *United States Investor, 9* (1898), 593.

9. J. W. Pratt, *Expansionists of 1898, the Acquisition of Hawaii and the Spanish Islands* (Baltimore, Johns Hopkins Press, 1936), pp. 252–253.

10. For an account of this institution see *Yearbook and Directory* of the Chamber of Commerce of Pittsburgh, 1898, pp. 44–52.

11. *Bradstreet's, 26* (1898), 818–819; *Public Opinion, 26* (1899), 29.

12. For the earlier history of the movement in so far as it related to China, see Rockhill papers (MSS in the Houghton Library, Harvard University), Rockhill to Roosevelt, September 24, 1895; *Proceedings of the Twenty-seventh Annual Meeting of the National Board of Trade*, January, 1897, pp. 65–79; *ibid., Twenty-eighth Annual Meeting*, December, 1897, p. 338; *Official Proceedings of the Ninth Session of the Trans-Mississippi Commercial Congress*, July, 1897, p. 310; *Fourth Spring Convention of the Merchants' Association of New York*, April, 1898, p. 39; *Asia; Journal of the American Asiatic Association, 1* (1898), 25.

13. On this matter see *Proceedings of the Thirtieth Annual Meeting of the National Board of Trade*, p. 289; *Fifty-first Annual Report of the Chamber of Commerce of San Francisco*, pp. 44, 71–72; *Journal of Commerce and Commercial Bulletin*, March 31, 1900; *Proceedings of the Fifth Annual Convention of the National Association of Manufacturers of the United States of America*, pp. 19–21; *Official Proceedings of the Eleventh Convention of the Trans-Mississippi Commercial Congress*, p. 302.

14. *Journal of Commerce and Commercial Bulletin*, January 13, 17, 26, 1899; *Fiftieth Annual Report of the Chamber of Commerce of San Francisco*, pp. 18–19; Boston Chamber of Commerce, *Annual Report* (1899), p. 114; Cleveland Chamber of Commerce, *Annual Report* (1899), p. 70; Rockhill papers, Chilton to Rockhill, February 1, 1899.

Many businessmen became so preoccupied with foreign commerce that they began to interpret the whole trend of international relations in terms of a world-wide struggle for markets. They envisaged all industrialized nations as caught in the iron grip of surplus production and consequently driven to a desperate search for markets. "Back of every political complication of today," one business publication asserted, "are trade considerations. Wars, treaties, colonization schemes and all the intricacies of diplomacy are really, in the final analysis, but means . . . of acquiring wealth." [15] "International politics," said another publication, "has simply become a series of questions relating to the development of trade." [16]

Such a conception of international relations, despite its Marxian flavor, prevailed in the most conservative circles. With a Darwinian admixture it was cherished by that epitome of everything safe, respectable, and orthodox, President McKinley himself. In his annual message of 1899 the president explained the doctrine to Congress:

In this age of keen rivalry among nations for mastery in commerce, the doctrine of evolution and the rule of the survival of the fittest must be as inexorable in their operation as they are positive in the results they bring about. The place won in the struggle by an industrial people can only be held by unrelaxed endeavor and constant advance in achievement.[17]

In many respects the conception was similar to the so-called Large Policy which took shape during the Spanish-American War. Proponents of the Large Policy such as A. T. Mahan, A. J. Beveridge, Henry Cabot Lodge, and Theodore Roosevelt believed that the United States had stayed at home too long; the time had long since come, they thought, for the country to step resolutely, in the full panoply of a great power, onto the international stage.[18] "For more than thirty years," wrote Henry Cabot Lodge as early as 1895, "we have been so much absorbed with grave domestic questions that we have lost sight of these vast interests which

15. *United States Investor, 9* (1898), 593.

16. *Journal of Commerce and Commercial Bulletin,* January 9, 1899.

17. *Papers Relating to the Foreign Relations of the United States with the Annual Message of the President Transmitted to Congress,* December 5, 1899 (Washington, 1901), p. xix. Hereafter cited as *Foreign Relations.*

18. For an account of the Large Policy see J. W. Pratt, "The 'Large Policy' of 1898," *Mississippi Valley Historical Review, 19* (1932), 219–242.

lie just outside of our borders." Like many a businessman he thought that "they ought to be neglected no longer." [19] Like many a businessman too, although with greater assurance, A. J. Beveridge in 1898 foresaw the destiny of America in glowing terms:

American factories are making more than the American people can use; American soil is producing more than they can consume. Fate has written our policy for us; the trade of the world must and shall be ours. And we will get it as our mother [England] has told us how. We will establish trading-posts throughout the world as distributing-points for American products. We will cover the ocean with our merchant marine. We will build a navy to the measure of our greatness. Great colonies governing themselves, flying our flag and trading with us, will grow about our posts of trade. Our institutions will follow our flag on the wings of our commerce. And American law, American order, American civilization, and the American flag will plant themselves on shores hitherto bloody and benighted, but by those agencies of God henceforth to be made beautiful and bright. [20]

Thus it was generally assumed that markets must be developed abroad. But why did businessmen single out China, as distinct from other markets, for special regard? Part of the answer lies in their fear that many foreign countries other than China were on the point of reducing imports from the United States.

Their concern was not altogether foolish. With American products capturing market after market some countries were becoming perturbed. "No question regarding commercial matters," a German publicist wrote in 1902, "was more often discussed in the old world, especially after the year 1898, than that of American competition." He added that people in Europe were beginning to speak not of American competition but of the American "spectre" or "invasion." The Yellow Peril, he declared, had a companion in the American Peril. [21] In Europe the characteristic reaction was

19. H. C. Lodge, "Our Blundering Foreign Policy," *The Forum, 19* (1895), 17.
20. C. G. Bowers, *Beveridge and the Progressive Era* (Cambridge, Houghton Mifflin Co., 1932), p. 69.
21. On this matter see M. Prager, "Die Amerikanische Gefahr," *Volkwirth-schaftliche Zeitfragen* (Berlin, 1902), p. 8. See also the anonymous article, "Two Presidents and the Limits of American Supremacy," *Fortnightly Review, 76* (1901), 558; C. Furness, "The Old World and the American 'Invasion,'" *Pall Mall Magazine, 26* (1902), 362–368; J. H. Clapham, *An Economic History of Modern Britain, Machines and National Rivalries (1887–1914), with an Epilogue (1914–1929)* (3 vols., Cambridge, 1926–38), III, 43–46.

advocacy of some sort of concerted commercial policy—perhaps even a customs union—directed against the United States. Although any such policy was impossible in the divided Europe of the time, it was talked about, and often in high places. Reports of the talk reached the United States and they excited apprehension.[22]

One of the most disturbing reports concerned an address delivered on November 20, 1897, by Count Goluchowski, minister of foreign affairs of Austria-Hungary. The count spoke in part as follows:

The destructive competition with transoceanic countries . . . requires prompt and thorough counteracting measures if vital interests of the peoples of Europe are not to be gravely compromised. They must fight shoulder to shoulder against the common danger, and must arm themselves for the struggle with all the means at their disposal. Just as the sixteenth and seventeenth centuries were absorbed by religious wars, as the eighteenth century was distinguished by the triumph of liberal ideas, and our own century by the appearance of nationality questions, in like manner the twentieth century would be, for Europe, a period marked by a struggle for existence in the politico-commercial sphere. The European nations must close their ranks in order successfully to defend their existence.[23]

Since everyone could see that the words "transoceanic countries" referred to the United States, the count's ominous exhortation to the nations of Europe to "close their ranks" led to much taking of counsel in America. Although the *Journal of Commerce* at first refused to be impressed (it insisted on America's "manifest destiny" to produce more than it could consume),[24] and the *Commercial and Financial Chronicle* consoled itself with the conjecture that Goluchowski's real purpose was to persuade his countrymen that plotting abroad was responsible for the depressed economic conditions at home,[25] by far the majority of American commentators showed real alarm. Never before, said United States Ambassador Tower at Vienna, had the suggestion of European union

---

22. F. Emory, "The United States in the World's Markets," *The Independent*, *53*, Part 3 (1901), 1542, reflects the American point of view. Emory was at one time chief of the Bureau of Foreign Commerce.

23. *Literary Digest, 15* (1897), 964.

24. *Journal of Commerce and Commercial Bulletin*, November 24, 1897.

25. *Commercial and Financial Chronicle, 65* (1897), 1147.

against America been put forward "so boldly" or by an official of "such importance." [26] In an editorial entitled "The European League," the *New York Times* warned Congress to give serious attention to the "extraordinary speech." [27] The *Times* pictured the country as helpless before European commercial attacks because rates of duty under the recent Dingley Tariff Act were already so high as to render ludicrous any threats of American retaliation.[28]

Particularly disturbing was the possibility that plans for resisting the United States might already be far advanced. From London, where Goluchowski's speech aroused the "most widespread interest," came word that the count would not have spoken without the approval of the continental governments; that he was, in fact, "the mouthpiece of those Governments." [29] The *Journal of Commerce* at once discarded its comfortable appeal to manifest destiny; Goluchowski, it now felt sure, was speaking for other countries as well as for Austria-Hungary. Russia was especially suspect. Was she not, the *Journal* asked, trying to stifle American trade in order to provide a market in Europe for the regions soon to be opened by the Trans-Siberian Railway? The *Journal* saw "unmistakable" signs of approaching discrimination against the United States.[30]

Germany too came in for suspicion. About three weeks after Goluchowski's speech Baron von Thielmann, secretary of the German Treasury and former ambassador to the United States, bluntly told the Reichstag that the Dingley Tariff Act put America in the position of a pike in a carp pond. The carp, he warned, must combine.[31] Von Thielmann may have been reflecting the opinion of the kaiser himself who, it is recorded, advised Europe in the summer of 1897 to unite in order "to shut out the transAtlantic competitor." [32] At any rate, Goluchowski and von Thielmann together convinced the American government that something was afoot. Immediately after von Thielmann's warning the State

26. A. Vagts, *Deutschland und die Vereinigten Staaten in der Weltpolitik* (2 vols., New York, Macmillan Co., 1935), I, 145, n. 1. Tower's statement was made November 24, 1897.

27. *New York Times*, November 23, 1897.

28. *Ibid.*, November 24, 1897.

29. *Ibid.*, November 22, 1897.

30. *Journal of Commerce and Commercial Bulletin*, November 30, 1897.

31. *New York Times*, December 13, 1897. Von Thielmann delivered his speech on December 10, 1897.

32. *The Memoirs of Count Witte* (London, 1921), pp. 407–410.

Department instructed Ambassador Tower at Vienna [33] and Ambassador White at Berlin [34] to watch the situation carefully; the "simultaneousness of these utterances in two such high quarters," Tower was told, "suggests a more than casual coincidence."

Far more disturbing to most American businessmen than unfriendly expressions from Austria-Hungary and Germany and suspicions of Russia were ominous pronouncements in Great Britain. At the height of the agitation over Goluchowski's call to arms Charles T. Ritchie, president of the Board of Trade, told the Croydon Chamber of Commerce that Britain's most dangerous trade rival was not Germany but the United States.[35] Particularly disquieting was the sustained campaign carried on by Joseph Chamberlain, in some ways the leading figure in the Cabinet, in favor of imperial preference. "A true Zollverein for the Empire," he told the Canada Club in 1896, ". . . although it would involve the imposition of duties against foreign countries . . . would still be a proper subject for discussion." [36] And a year later in a speech to the Colonial Conference he made a similar suggestion: if a complete customs union was impractical at the moment the colonies could at least give preferential treatment to the mother country.[37] Whether customs union or preferential system, the effect on the United States, in accepted opinion, would be reduced exports and hence a mounting surplus with all its dreaded consequences.

A discriminatory commercial policy on the part of continental countries would be serious enough; on the part of Great Britain it would be calamitous. Britain was America's chief market. Moreover, any new British policy would in all probability carry along her whole empire and, in consequence of her key position in international commerce, many independent countries as well. There loomed before American traders the ugly prospect of a drastic reduction in exports to much of Asia, more of Africa, and almost all of Europe. The only substantial markets still available would be South America and China. As between the two most businessmen regarded the latter as by all odds the more valuable. From the Civil War to 1900 exports from the United States to South

33. Department of State, Instructions, Austria, *4*, 302–303, Sherman to Tower, December 14, 1897.

34. *Ibid.*, Germany, *20*, 293–294, Sherman to White, December 14, 1897.

35. *New York Times*, November 24, 1897.

36. J. L. Garvin, *The Life of Joseph Chamberlain* (3 vols., London, Macmillan & Co., 1932–34), III, 180; speech to Canada Club, March 25, 1896.

37. *Ibid.*, III, 191–192; speech of July 5, 1897.

America had fallen off—quite in contrast to exports to China. Furthermore South America, like Europe, was thought to be meditating a combination to fence off the United States.[38] The "struggle for commercial supremacy of the world is to be waged in Eastern Asia and not in South America," said the *Journal of Commerce*.[39] Undoubtedly it was expressing the prevailing opinion. China alone remained.

Thus, partly because they feared a surplus at home and discrimination abroad, large numbers of businessmen came to think of China as the great hope of the future. But their expectations were not based exclusively on negative considerations. This market of last resort might also be potentially the greatest market in the world. Their faith in its potentialities did more than their dread of a surplus to prepare the ground for the Open Door Policy.

38. *Literary Digest, 17* (1898), 113.
39. *Journal of Commerce and Commercial Bulletin*, January 12, 1899.

II

THE POTENTIAL MARKET

THE belief in the great potentialities of the Chinese market although widespread in the United States in the 1890's had little rational basis. Nevertheless businessmen from time to time sought support for their hopes in statistics showing exports to China.

Under the most-favored-nation treatment which China accorded the United States in the treaty of Wanghia, 1844, exports from America to China increased rapidly, from $2,276,000 in 1845 to $8,906,000 in 1860.[1] With the Civil War came a change; exports fell and for the next thirty years or so languished. Increasing competition from Japan, depreciation of silver (the base of China's currency) in terms of gold, Chinese animosity over America's immigration policy, decline of the United States merchant marine, and, above all, absorption of productive capacity in the development of the American West were the principal reasons for the decline. But in the 1890's when the surplus appeared the spotlight shifted from the West to foreign markets; and exports to China, sharing in the general expansion, were soon larger than ever before. Between 1890 and 1900 they increased from $7,385,362 to $23,745,000. The figures for total American exports to all parts of the world during the same two years were $857,502,548 and $1,478,050,000 respectively.[2]

1. S. L. Pan, *The Trade of the United States with China* (New York, 1924), has material on this earlier period.

2. *Exports from the United States to China*

Year Ending June 30	U.S. Dollars
1890	7,385,362
1891	13,469,687
1892	10,557,546
1893	8,117,059
1894	10,072,273
1895	7,856,880
1896	11,613,134

Although exports to China accounted for a negligible percentage of total exports throughout the 1890's, they increased during the decade by over 200 per cent, a far larger increase than to any other area except Africa. And since most of Africa had been partitioned among the great powers of Europe it was written off as a future market for the United States. The rise in exports to China impressed many Americans. If China could treble her purchase of goods in a decade, why should she not repeat this in succeeding decades? The increase also impressed Europeans. Back from a trip to the Far East an English mining expert, C. A. Moreing, pointed to the flourishing American export trade with China. "This development," he predicted, "is still in its infancy." [3]

Thus a great number of Americans, worried about overproduction, came to envisage the Chinese Empire as a unique country offering "simply incalculable" possibilities for commerce and po-

1897	17,984,472
1898	16,258,094
1899	22,225,965
1900	23,745,000

This table is adapted from F. H. Hitchcock, *Our Trade with Japan, China, and Hongkong, 1889–1899* (Washington, 1900), and Pan, *Trade of the United States with China*. The figures include exports to Hongkong, which as a British Crown Colony was outside the application of the Open Door notes. But since a large percentage of most goods exported to Hongkong was re-exported to China, it would be misleading to exclude exports to Hongkong entirely from consideration. Therefore in speaking of exports to China it will be understood that Hongkong is included, but it should be kept in mind that the figures are a little larger than if they related to China only.

Exports from the United States, 1890 and 1900
(U.S. dollars)

To	1890 (calendar year)	1900 (calendar year)
Europe	682,585,856	1,111,456,000
North America	95,517,863	202,486,000
South America	34,722,122	41,384,000
Asia	22,854,028	60,598,000
Oceania	17,375,745	39,956,000
Africa	4,446,934	22,170,000
Total	857,502,548	1,478,050,000

This table is from *Commercial Relations of the United States with Foreign Countries during the Year 1900* (2 vols., Washington, 1901), I, 37. Hereafter cited as *Commercial Relations*.

Although the same years in the tables relate to different twelve-month periods, the comparison in the text between figures taken from the two tables is exact enough for present purposes.

3. C. A. Moreing, "A Recent Business Tour in China," *The Nineteenth Century and After*, 44 (1898), 397.

tentially "the greatest of the world markets." [4] So often did people
allude to its tremendous population that four hundred million became a figure almost magical in its anticipated effect on exports.
"In China there are four hundred millions of people, more than
five times as many as exist in the United States. The wants of
these four hundred millions are increasing every year. What a
market!" [5] Eager statisticians estimated that if only every person
in China consumed even a single bushel of flour a year the "entire
American crop would be wanted . . ." [6] or if each of the Chinese
bought just one biscuit a day American factories would have to
run day and night to meet the demand.[7] It was "none too soon,"
warned the *Iron Age*, for the United States to realize the implica-
tions of facing the Pacific as well as the Atlantic.[8] According to
the National Association of Manufacturers trade with China was
"only in its early stages" and had "enormous possibilities"; it
could furnish a market for "millions upon millions of dollars' worth
of American products." [9] The "most intelligent and enterprising
methods" should be used to develop it, asserted the Boston Chamber
of Commerce; [10] and the San Francisco chamber greeted the "vast
opportunities" in Oriental commerce.[11] "Vast" was not strong
enough for the president of the Chicago Board of Trade or for
Bradstreet's. To the one, the opportunities were "such as were
never presented to any other nation"; [12] to the other, they seemed
"the greatest . . . which manufacturing nations have ever enjoyed." [13] If only China could be kept open to American exports,
thought the *Journal of Commerce*, "the serious problem—where
can we find markets for our prospective surplus of manufactures?
—would be in no small measure solved." [14] Even the surplus would
melt away before the growing market across the Pacific.

Prevalent beliefs about China's future capacity to absorb the
American industrial surplus were often apparent in business

4. *Journal of Commerce and Commercial Bulletin*, January 8, 1898.

5. *Banker and Tradesman and Massachusetts Law Reporter, 24* (1898), 776.

6. *Official Proceedings of the Ninth Session of the Trans-Mississippi Commercial Congress*, July, 1897, p. 251.

7. *Literary Digest, 19* (1899), 607.

8. *Iron Age, 61* (1898), 17.

9. *Senate Report*, No. 450, 56th Congress, First Session, p. 8.

10. Boston Chamber of Commerce, *Annual Report* (1900), p. 130.

11. *Fiftieth Annual Report of the Chamber of Commerce of San Francisco*, p. 23.

12. Chicago Board of Trade, *Forty-second Annual Report* (1899), p. xxxviii.

13. *Bradstreet's, 27* (1899), 451.

14. *Journal of Commerce and Commercial Bulletin*, December 28, 1897.

analyses of foreign policy. If the writers expected a particular policy to promote exports to China, more often than not they favored it; if they expected the contrary, they were apt to oppose it. In discussions of even the most hallowed American traditions this bias often showed itself. The *United States Investor* was quite prepared to forsake the advice of Washington's Farewell Address:

Washington's policy is not one to be abandoned without the gravest cause. But that it will be abandoned eventually and on justifiable grounds, seems to us highly profitable [*sic*]. . . . Putting sentimental considerations entirely one side, the commercial relations of the American people are fast assuming a character which will make it hard to keep from intervening in the affairs of the other hemisphere [that is, Eastern Asia].[15]

John R. Proctor, president of the Civil Service Commission, suggested an amendment to another cherished policy, the Monroe Doctrine: let it be expanded to cover China as well as the New World.[16]

It was particularly in connection with current issues of foreign policy pressing for settlement in the late 1890's that the stress on the Chinese market made itself felt. The principal issue before the American people early in 1898 was whether or not to fight Spain; but at times commentators subordinated even this paramount question to that of exporting to China. Thus the New Orleans *Times Picayune* complained that the government was thinking altogether too much about difficulties with the Spaniards and not enough about the country's stake in China.[17] Such complaints were not typical, but their appearing in print at all is significant in view of the emotionalism pervading the controversy with Spain.

Another major question was whether or not the United States should dig a Central American canal. One of the most frequent arguments advanced by proponents maintained that a canal, by

15. *United States Investor, 9* (1898), 593.
16. He suggested the following additional article: Although the United States does not take part in purely European affairs, "with the movements in China we are of necessity more intimately connected. . . . We owe it, therefore, to candor and to the amicable relations existing between the United States and . . . [European] powers to declare that we should consider any attempt on their part to extend their system to any portion of the Chinese Empire as dangerous to our peace and safety, and as a manifestation of an unfriendly disposition towards the United States." *Harper's Weekly, 63* (1899), 1179.
17. Cited in *Literary Digest, 16* (1898), 33. There is a large number of similar expressions in the same issue.

cutting transportation costs, would enable the country to compete more effectively in the Orient. There were at the time two commonly used all-water routes from New York to Shanghai: by the Cape of Good Hope, 14,340 nautical miles, and by Suez, 12,360 nautical miles. The land-and-water route by train to the Pacific coast and thence by ship, although shorter, was particularly expensive for the bulky, low-priced goods that constituted the largest part of American exports to the Orient. But with a canal at Panama or elsewhere in Central America the distance from New York to Shanghai would be only 10,640 nautical miles, and from New Orleans just under 10,000 nautical miles, almost exactly what it was from Plymouth, England. Furthermore, because fewer storm areas would normally be encountered on the route via Central America than by way of either Suez or the Cape, a canal would lower insurance rates, thereby still further improving the competitive position of American exporters.

Cotton interests, especially in the South, figured prominently among those advocating a waterway across Central America. As early as 1892 the Houston *Trade-Review* was proclaiming a canal to be of vital significance to the South on the ground that it would promote cotton exports to China.[18] Some years later this point had a leading place on the agenda of a cotton convention in Atlanta; [19] it was the subject of a careful study published by the New Orleans Board of Trade; [20] and according to *Bradstreet's* it had become one of the most frequently heard arguments for construction.[21] A canal, people believed, would help American cotton in another way. At present, so ran the argument, exporters could ship raw cotton to England for manufacture without adding appreciably to the total mileage to the Far East; but once water shipment by way of Central America became possible, transportation costs would be so much lower than by way of England that a premium would be placed on manufacture in the United States.[22] Thus the American cotton textile industry would benefit.

18. Cited in *Dixie, a Monthly Record of Southern Industrial Possibility and Developments, 3* (1892), 19.

19. *Bradstreet's, 27* (1899), 689.

20. New Orleans Board of Trade, Limited, *Correspondence, Reports, and Addresses on the Subject of the Commercial and Industrial Value of an Inter-oceanic Canal* (1900).

21. *Bradstreet's, 28* (1900), 116.

22. See the New Orleans Board of Trade, Limited, *Correspondence, Reports, and Addresses;* Department of State, Despatches, Shanghai, *46,* Goodnow to Hill, December 23, 1899.

The whole Mississippi River Valley too expected to share in increased trade with China.[23] In its opinion that the "increasing importance" of this trade "necessitates" early construction the Merchants' Exchange of St. Louis was representative of much sentiment in the area.[24]

Probably the most important issue of foreign policy once the decision had been taken to fight Spain was that of overseas expansion. Before the war businessmen did not in general advocate the acquisition of colonies as a means of extending markets. Instead, they put their trust in world-wide lowering of tariffs, at least on the part of countries other than the United States.[25] In this anti-imperialistic point of view they differed, of course, from enthusiasts for the Large Policy who even before the war favored overseas expansion. But when Goluchowski, Chamberlain, and others brought up the possibility of concerted action to restrict American exports they dealt a severe blow to hopes of tariff reduction. Such dreams seemed all the more naïve after Japan, Russia, France, Germany, and Great Britain, noting Chinese weakness in the Sino-Japanese War of 1894–95, carved out for themselves in China spheres of influence and economic concessions of one kind or another. Consequently, when Admiral Dewey's victory over the Spanish fleet at Manila Bay, May 1, 1898, suddenly made American imperialism a very immediate issue, many businessmen swung over to the gospel of expansion. Nowhere is the metamorphosis of outlook more strikingly illustrated than in the columns of the New York *Journal of Commerce and Commercial Bulletin.* Throughout the early 1890's this newspaper consistently preached tariff reduction; but in the course of a few weeks following the outburst of European imperialistic activity in China it threw its old faith to the winds and emerged a vociferous and determined advocate of American imperialism. The *Journal's* conversion resulted from sudden awareness of danger to the Chinese market. China must be saved for the surplus products of American industries.

The discussion of expansion centered on whether to annex the Philippine Islands. Businessmen came to favor annexation because they thought it would insure continued access to China. Mark

23. *Official Proceedings of the Eleventh Convention of the Trans-Mississippi Commercial Congress,* April, 1900, considers this matter.

24. *Annual Statement of the Trade and Commerce of Saint Louis for the Year 1900, Reported to the Merchants' Exchange of St. Louis* (St. Louis, 1901), p. 26.

25. Pratt, *Expansionists of 1898,* chap. vii.

Hanna, consistent exponent of business ideals and leading figure
in the Republican party, sounded the prevailing opinion when he
said: ". . . with a strong foothold in the Philippine Islands . . .
we can and will take a large slice of the commerce of Asia. That
is what we want. We are bound to share in the commerce of the
Far East, and it is better to strike for it while the iron is hot." [26]
There was no sectional division; all the country over, the larger
part of articulate business opinion favored taking the islands. In
the East the American Asiatic Association considered annexation
essential to the "commercial interests of our citizens in the Far
East." [27] An enthusiastic speaker told the Connecticut State Board
of Trade that the Philippines would bring "unparalleled benefit"
to the United States; they would hold open "the gates of trade
with the great East . . . with its teeming millions of people." He
added significantly: ". . . the future looks bright for our manufacturing industries to find a market for their surplus goods." [28]
To a southern publication the Philippines were an "indispensable
base" for trade with eastern Asia, the only market big enough for
cotton.[29] According to the Chicago *Times Herald* mid-western
commercial and industrial interests, impressed by the proximity
of the islands to the "vast . . . markets of the Orient," were
pleading "Keep the Philippines." [30] And on the Pacific coast three
San Francisco business organizations [31]—the Chamber of Commerce, the Merchants' Association, and the Manufacturers' and
Producers' Association—together with the Seattle Chamber of
Commerce [32] petitioned President McKinley to retain the Philippines in order to strengthen trade relations with the Orient.

Closely associated with the issue of the Philippines was the
question of annexing Hawaii, which was often thought of merely
as a halfway station to the Philippines. While the Philippines were
required to safeguard the potential Chinese market, Hawaii was
required to safeguard the Philippines. Senator G. F. Hoar in his
autobiography writes: "Several very distinguished gentlemen
indeed . . . were urging publicly and privately the Hawaiian

26. *World* (New York), August 29, 1898.

27. *Asia; Journal of the American Asiatic Association, 1* (1898), 1.

28. *Proceedings of the Connecticut State Board of Trade, 1891–1906,* Ninth Annual Meeting, October 19, 1898.

29. *Tradesman* of Chattanooga; cited in *Literary Digest, 18* (1898), 361.

30. Cited in *Literary Digest, 17* (1898), 33.

31. *Forty-ninth Annual Report of the Chamber of Commerce of San Francisco,*
pp. 23–24.

32. *Literary Digest, 17* (1898), 241.

Treaty on the ground that we must have Hawaii in order to help us get our share of China." [33] One of the "distinguished gentlemen" was Hoar's colleague, William P. Frye, an influential senator who served on the commission to make peace with Spain. As early as January, 1898, Senator Frye favored Hawaiian annexation because "the whole world will accept that as the first step in the direction of exercising our moral influence to preserve the integrity of China." [34]

A cable across the Pacific would also serve to promote trade with the Far East. Hence a cable was widely favored, often in conjunction with recommendations of Hawaiian and Philippine annexation. "As the United States proposes to control the Pacific Ocean, as the United States will retain the Philippines, develop trade with China, and construct the canal, as the United States intends to build up a merchant marine and support that service with a great navy, is it not proper that the United States should lay down the Pacific cable?" asked the *Philadelphia Inquirer*. "We think it is," came the not surprising reply.[35] In the far West, where interest was strong, the San Francisco Chamber of Commerce found a cable required "not alone on the ground of national policy, but with equal if not greater urgency by the demands of commerce." [36]

Canal, overseas expansion, and cable—here were three issues of the 1890's with which businessmen concerned themselves, in large measure because of their esteem for the market in China.[37] The Southern Cotton Spinners' Association, meeting in Charlotte, South Carolina, in the autumn of 1899, adopted a resolution urging the government to preserve the Chinese Empire, to construct an Isthmian canal, to maintain permanent control over the Philippines, and to lay down a Pacific cable. The conclusion of the resolution provides an excellent example of the tendency to subordinate many issues of foreign policy, however vital in themselves, to the overriding desire to save China for American exports: "We consider that a large degree of the importance of the last

33. G. F. Hoar, *Autobiography of Seventy Years* (2 vols., New York, 1902), II, 308.

34. *Philadelphia Press*, January 5, 1898.

35. Cited in *Literary Digest, 20* (1900), 233. See also *ibid.*, p. 177.

36. *Fiftieth Annual Report of the Chamber of Commerce of San Francisco*, pp. 8–9. For similar observations see *ibid.*, p. 18; *Iron Age, 62* (1898), 21; Minute-Book of the American Asiatic Association, 1898–1919 (MS in the offices of the association, 55 Wall Street, New York), p. 3; *Congressional Record, 32*, 769.

37. *Literary Digest, 20* (1900), 177.

three items lies in the value of those measures in accomplishing the first item and in protecting our trade in China." [38]

Thus there is no lack of evidence that businessmen in the late 1890's paid close attention to developments affecting the Chinese market. Impressed by its supposed commercial possibilities and fearing overproduction at home and discrimination abroad, they believed that retention and cultivation of the market across the Pacific were essential to the continued prosperity of the United States. This belief helped to produce a set of conditions favorable to the despatch of the Open Door notes in 1899 and 1900.

Besides those who were looking mainly to the future there were businessmen who already had dealings with China. Naturally their interest in China was more immediate and direct than that of men who, without present involvement, were thinking about the hopes and dangers of years to come. More effectively than all the persons dreaming of the potential market, the men hard at work in the actual market helped to bring about the Open Door Policy.

38. *Journal of Commerce and Commercial Bulletin*, November 3, 1899.

III

THE ACTUAL MARKET

O F ALL American businesses operating in the Chinese Empire in the 1890's, two by far surpassed the others in amount of financial involvement: the cotton-goods industry and the American-China Development Company (a concern seeking railway concessions). Since the most effective business pressure for a strong Far Eastern policy came from these two special interests they merit close attention.

Exports of the cotton-goods industry consisted, in the main, of plain gray and white goods.[1]

Imports into China of Plain Gray and White Cotton Goods [2]

From	1887		1897	
	Pieces	U.S. Dollars	Pieces	U.S. Dollars
England	11,037,745	18,335,512	9,114,374	16,507,168
India			404,724	380,560
United States	1,874,274	5,331,251	4,143,971	8,500,802
Netherlands	82,635	178,114	76,752	125,312
Japan	—	—	286,480	216,559
Total	12,994,654	23,844,877	14,026,301	25,730,401

1. Americans did not send China appreciable amounts of raw cotton until 1898 when they exported 5,650,856 pounds valued at $370,670. Exports to China of all kinds of manufactured cottons were only slightly greater than exports of the one category, plain gray and white goods. Exports from the United States to China of all manufactured cottons were as follows:

Year Ending June 30	U.S. Dollars
1890	1,252,859
1891	5,360,508
1892	3,934,705
1893	1,667,929
1894	2,870,765
1895	1,741,942
1896	4,077,254
1897	7,489,141
1898	5,243,885

(Statistics in this footnote are from *Commercial Relations* [1898], I, 13.)

2. *Consular Reports* (Washington, 1899), *59,* chart following p. 560. In the table in the text the figure $8,500,802 for 1897 relates to but one kind of manufactured

As a supplier of plain gray and white goods the United States, while second to England, was making greater headway than other countries. From 1887 to 1897 American exports to China of these cottons increased by 121 per cent in quantity and 59 per cent in value, whereas exports from England and all other leading suppliers decreased in both categories. It appeared to contemporaries that the United States was capturing the Chinese market, after India the world's largest for cotton goods.[3]

China alone purchased nearly half of all American exports of cottons; the second largest importer took only about one-fourth as much.[4] The American industry thus depended to a marked degree on its market in China. Particularly dependent were the mills in the southern states, where many establishments staked their "very existence" on this distant market.[5] "You can at once see what the importance of the China trade is to us," a convention of cotton spinners of South Carolina wrote their congressmen in 1899. "It is everything. The prosperity of the cotton-mill business of South Carolina depends in our opinion upon the China trade." [6]

The cotton-goods industry, especially in the South, was progressing rapidly in the 1890's. From 1889 to 1900 the number of southern spindles increased by 194 per cent (from 1,360,000 to 4,000,000), as against an increase of 11 per cent in the North, 71 per cent in India, 30 per cent on the continent of Europe, and 4 per cent in Great Britain.[7] Yet manufacturers were worried. Nearly all their exports went to parts of China which seemed particularly endangered by foreign domination, namely, north China and Manchuria. The United States was easily the leading supplier of cotton goods to those areas; [8] but Russian influence was growing steadily, and Americans feared that the day was close

cotton, whereas in the table in n. 1 the figure for 1897, $7,489,141, though smaller, relates to all kinds of manufactured cottons. The explanation of the apparent discrepancy is that the former figure relates to the calendar year, the latter to the year ending June 30.

3. R. M. Odell, *Cotton Goods in China* (Washington, 1916), United States Bureau of Foreign and Domestic Commerce, Special Agents Series, No. 107, p. 5.

4. The figures have been compiled from *Commercial Relations* (1899), Vol. I.

5. *Transactions of the New England Cotton Manufacturers' Association*, No. 69, p. 319.

6. *Senate Document*, No. 230, 56th Congress, First Session, pp. 6–7. For similar observations see *Bradstreet's, 26* (1898), 113; *27* (1899), 689; *Journal of Commerce and Commercial Bulletin*, June 16, October 16, and November 3, 1899.

7. *Commercial Relations* (1900), I, 38.

8. See *Accounts and Papers, Africa to China* (1900), No. 2369, where the British Consul in Newchwang laments American predominance.

when Russia would be able to reserve the markets for herself.

The cotton interests were all the more apprehensive because of a painful injury which Russia's ally France had recently inflicted upon their commerce with Madagascar. For some years American exports of cotton goods to that French colony had been more valuable than those of any other country; in the interior, in fact, they had enjoyed a near monopoly. Various other nations had striven to get the trade, but to no avail.[9] This pleasant situation changed abruptly in 1897. In August France put into effect in Madagascar a new tariff giving preference to herself; moreover, in order further to promote the purchase of French goods she began to use what an American observer termed "peculiar methods." [10] In consequence exports from the United States fell sharply. Whereas in 1897 the island imported American cottons valued at $431,688, two years later imports amounted to a mere $245. Over the same period the value of French cottons brought into Madagascar rose from $97,340 to $1,542,858.[11]

The American business press often cited the collapse of this once promising market as an object lesson of what to expect should China likewise find herself one day at the mercy of a colonial power. For cotton exporters the lesson was all too clear: their precious market in north China and Manchuria could easily become another Madagascar. Faced by a prospective loss that would mean ruin, men connected with the cotton industry were among the most fervent and persistent advocates of governmental action in support of the Open Door in China.

The other leading American business operating in China was the American-China Development Company. Established in 1895, the company by 1899 had a capital of $1,000,000.[12] Among its shareholders it numbered men foremost in the business world: [13] Calvin S. Brice, the company's first president and former senator from Ohio; Thomas C. Platt, senator from New York; Levi P. Morton, a New York lawyer, formerly vice-president of the United States under Benjamin Harrison; Frederick P. Olcott, president

9. *Commercial Relations* (1895–96), I, 94.

10. *Ibid.* (1898), I, 223; and (1899), I, 253. The new tariff was dated August 26, 1897.

11. *Ibid.* (1900), I, 294.

12. Department of State, Miscellaneous Letters, May, 1898, Part 1, filed under May 3.

13. For the complete list of shareholders see *ibid.*, July, 1899, Part 2, filed under July 13; also *ibid.*, August, 1898, Part 2, filed under August 19.

of the Central Trust Company of New York; John I. Waterbury, president of the Manhattan Trust Company; James Stillman, president of the National City Bank (who also represented Rockefeller interests); George F. Baker, president of the First National Bank of New York; Charles Coster, of J. P. Morgan and Company; Jacob H. Schiff, of Kuhn, Loeb and Company; E. H. Harriman, chairman of the executive committee of the Union Pacific Railway; and G. R. Hegeman, president of the Metropolitan Life Insurance Company. Other shareholders were the American Sugar Refineries Company, the Carnegie Steel Company, and several railway companies. One man deserves particular notice: Clarence Cary, a New York lawyer who was the company's legal adviser and one of its largest stockholders.[14] Few men worked more diligently or with greater effect than Cary to bring about a change in Far Eastern policy.

The American-China Development Company existed for the purpose of acquiring railway concessions in China. In this desire it represented an exception to the general American trend as regards investing abroad. At the beginning of 1899, $3,330,000,000 of foreign capital was invested in the United States, while only $500,000,000 of American capital was invested abroad.[15] The United States was still, on balance, a capital-importing nation. Consequently, in marked contrast to the widespread interest in trade with China, few Americans wished to intrust their money to that country.[16] At the close of the nineteenth century they had invested only $17,500,000 in China as compared with $150,000,000 in Europe and $185,000,000 in Mexico.[17] But the Development Company had no regard for the prevailing trend and eagerly sought to put its resources in China. Its influential shareholders included earnest proponents of whatever measures might be necessary to keep China accessible to American commerce and capital.

14. *Ibid.*, July, 1899, Part 2, filed under July 13. The same source describes Cary as holding some shares for "the Vanderbilt party."

15. N. T. Bacon, "American International Indebtedness," *Yale Review, 9* (1900), 265–285. Although she was not a net exporter of capital, there were "signs . . . that America was bounding ahead as a financial power," according to C. K. Hobson, *The Export of Capital* (London, 1914), p. 153.

16. Again and again American diplomatic and consular representatives in China deplored what seemed to them mere stubborn refusal to reap sure profits. For some of their laments see *Consular Reports, 59,* 445, and *61,* 307; *Commercial Relations* (1896–97), I, 173 and *ibid.* (1898), I, 130; Vagts, *Deutschland und die Vereinigten Staaten,* II, 1036–1038.

17. C. F. Remer, *Foreign Investments in China* (New York, 1933), p. 260; Bacon, "American International Indebtedness," *Yale Review, 9* (1900), 276.

Like the cotton-goods industry, the American-China Development Company was a determined advocate of a vigorous policy in the Far East.

Certain other businesses, although having smaller sums of money at stake, likewise had good reason to agitate for support of the Open Door. Next to cotton goods the most valuable American exports to China in the 1890's were kerosene, wheat flour, and iron and steel manufactures. During the decade exports of kerosene fluctuated in value from just under $2,000,000 in 1895 to nearly $4,500,000 in 1897.[18] These amounts were not impressive as compared with the industry's total exports, but American oil interests, optimistic about future possibilities if the door could be kept open, were anxious to maintain their foothold in China.[19]

Exports of wheat flour to China reached their greatest value, $134,969, in 1891; for all other years of the 1890's except one (1895) they were below $100,000.[20] Although the figures were small, they did not discourage enthusiasts who, hoping to convert the Chinese from rice to wheat, saw almost limitless possibilities ahead. As one such visionary prophesied: "Once let it [flour] become a common article of diet among these many millions of people and this country [the United States] will have a handy market for its entire surplus." [21]

Similarly, exports of iron and steel goods to China reached a top value of $132,188 in 1898.[22] Many manufacturers believed that as soon as large-scale construction of Chinese railways commenced

18. Adapted from Hitchcock, *Our Trade with Japan, China and Hongkong.* Further statistics adapted from the same source, showing American exports to China of kerosene, follow:

Year Ending June 30	Gallons	U.S. Dollars
1890	24,222,220	2,388,456
1891	37,975,290	3,626,529
1892	33,900,390	2,553,595
1893	40,633,050	2,648,237
1894	57,266,116	3,455,461
1895	28,618,410	1,994,449
1896	36,193,890	3,034,850
1897	57,493,170	4,492,973
1898	59,961,764	3,805,862

19. See *Accounts and Papers, Africa to China* (1900), No. 2499; *Commercial Relations* (1899), I, 71.

20. *Commercial Relations* (1898), I, 15.

21. *Official Proceedings of the Ninth Session of the Trans-Mississippi Commercial Congress,* July, 1897, p. 251.

22. *Commercial Relations* (1898), I, 15.

a splendid market for American iron and steel would develop.[23]

Finally, there were certain American firms, several with headquarters in Shanghai, which acted as middlemen in Chinese-American commerce. [24] Should discriminatory commercial policies arise in China such firms would probably face bankruptcy. Consequently many of them became zealous champions of American intervention in support of the Open Door.

The American-China Development Company, the cotton-goods industry, and to a less extent the oil, flour, and iron and steel businesses, and the trading houses, were the special business interests which had the largest amounts of money, present and prospective, involved in their operations in China. Should measures discriminatory to American investment and commerce become effective there the flour, iron and steel, and oil industries would suffer losses; while the Development Company, many cotton mills, and the trading houses would be forced to curtail operations drastically. The general business community, moreover, would no longer be able to bank on its cherished potential market. With so much at stake many businessmen would be sure to rally to the defense of China if ever she should be endangered. In the late 1890's serious threats to the safety of China did, in fact, arise. The stage was thus set for the beginnings of business pressure on Washington.

23. With respect to these exports the situation was complicated by the existence of another "potential" market in the Far East, namely, Siberia. Exporters of iron and steel to Siberia were naturally inclined to view Russian encroachments into Manchuria and southward in quite a different light from exporters to China. Thus, even though iron and steel goods constituted one of the leading American exports to China, there was a division within the industry as to whether or not the United States should take a strong stand for the Open Door (Vagts, *Deutschland und die Vereinigten Staaten,* I, 346; II, 1041).

24. Among the firms with headquarters in China were the American Trading Co.; the China and Japan Trading Co.; Fearon, Daniel and Co.; Frazar and Co.; Macy and Co.; Shewan, Tomes and Co.; Wheelock and Co.; Wisner and Co.; L. H. Smith and Co.; Clarkson and Co. Among those with headquarters in the United States were Bliss, Fabyan and Co.; Deering, Milliken and Co.; Charles A. Schieren and Co.; A. Norden and Co.; Catlin and Co.; Seeger and Guernsey; Smith, Hogg and Gardner; Busk and Jevons; E. D. Cordes and Co.; Minot, Hooper and Co.; Geo. W. Lane and Co.; Woodward, Baldwin and Co.; Wheelwright, Eldredge and Co.; the Pepperell Manufacturing Co.

IV

ORGANIZATION OF A PROPAGANDA

BY THE beginning of 1898 a number of businessmen connected with the cotton industry, with the American-China Development Company, and with certain other enterprises had become convinced of the need, if the Chinese market was to be kept open, of fundamental changes in United States policy. Various Far Eastern developments converging toward a crisis helped produce among these men a growing sense of urgency.

One such development was the rapidly increasing momentum of enchroachments by European countries upon the Chinese Empire. In March, 1897, France persuaded China to agree never to cede the island of Hainan to any other country. Germany in November, 1897, landed troops at Kiaochao, a port in Shantung Province which for some time she had been considering as a naval base. More alarming still was the news of a Russian fleet dropping anchor at Port Arthur. Occupation of this strategic center would enable Russia not only to strengthen her hold on the immense areas of China already subject to her influence but—what might prove even more serious—to command the sea approaches to Peking itself.[1] The delicate balance of the great powers in China seemed on the point of collapse, and in all probability the extinction of Chinese independence would follow. The gloomy prospect greatly disturbed many Americans. The minister to China, Charles Denby, considered the situation so serious that he advised immediate, full-fledged intervention in the Orient. Partition, he declared, would destroy America's market in China,[2] "the greatest market of the world." [3]

1. For details of the Kiaochao and Port Arthur incidents see P. Joseph, *Foreign Diplomacy in China, 1894–1900, a Study in Political and Economic Relations with China* (London, 1928), chaps. ix, xi; and W. L. Langer, *The Diplomacy of Imperialism, 1890–1902* (2 vols., New York, A. A. Knopf, and London, 1935), Vol. II, chap. xiv.

2. Department of State, Despatches, China, *103*, No. 2858, Denby to Sherman, January 31, 1898.

3. *Ibid.,* Denby to Sherman, February 14, 1898.

Like Minister Denby the special business interests saw much reason for concern. Nowhere is their anxiety more evident than in the New York *Journal of Commerce*—of all American newspapers, it is safe to say, the most fervent prophet of a glorious future in China for American business. Ever since the beginnings of the Kiaochao and Port Arthur affairs the *Journal* had been printing editorial after editorial stressing the urgency of action to safeguard the Chinese market. Once the kaiser and the tsar controlled China, the *Journal* proclaimed confidently, they would show other countries the "least possible consideration." [4] Just why this particular newspaper became so obsessed with China is not certain. Various explanations are possible: a regular contributor, Charles A. Conant, was a well-known expounder of the tenets of the Large Policy; [5] an editor, John Foord (one of the leading figures in the history of the Open Door Policy), busied himself with efforts to strengthen Far Eastern policy; and the paper carried a great deal of advertising by cotton interests. Whatever the significance of this last point, it is a striking fact that the *Journal of Commerce* watched tirelessly over the interests in China of the American cotton industry and faithfully expounded the industry's point of view. It reported with evident satisfaction that the great trading houses of New York, several of which handled the thriving cotton-goods trade with China, realized the need in the critical period at the end of 1897 to "arouse the Administration" to a defense of American interests in the Far East. [6]

Like the *Journal of Commerce* and the cotton industry the American-China Development Company was disquieted over the course of events and saw every reason to put pressure on Washington. Although it still, despite nearly three years of effort, had no concession, the company harbored most ambitious designs: a railway running through the heart of China from Canton to Hankow to Peking, going on to Manchuria and then through the entire length of that province, and finally joining the Trans-Siberian Railway. Shortly after the company's formation in 1895 its special agent in China, A. W. Bash, sought Minister Denby's help. [7] Denby, impressed by the company's roster of eminent share-

4. *Journal of Commerce and Commercial Bulletin,* December 28, 1897.
5. A collection of Conant's articles putting forth this point of view is entitled *The United States in the Orient, the Nature of the Economic Problem* (Boston and New York, 1900). The articles originally appeared in leading periodicals.
6. *Journal of Commerce and Commercial Bulletin,* December 29 and 31, 1897.
7. Vagts, *Deutschland und die Vereinigten Staaten,* II, 962.

holders,[8] was the more anxious to assist because he himself had formerly been in the railway business in the United States.[9] Accordingly, he requested of the State Department authorization to select an American concern (presumably the Development Company) and to "advocate its interests and secure contracts, etc." [10] But the secretary of state, Richard Olney, was opposed to such evident favoritism and refused the request.

Not long after conferring with Denby Bash called upon Count Cassini, the tsar's envoy to China. He assured the count of the company's resolve not to act in Manchuria without Russia's full approval.[11] But Russia, expecting to be well-nigh impregnable there once the Trans-Siberian Railway was completed, had no intention of allowing a foreign company to exploit a region which she had marked out for her own.[12] Bash, as it happened, was negotiating in regard to Manchuria with China too,[13] but he had no chance of success against Russian opposition. Accepting the inevitable, the company finally turned its attention southward.[14]

Here prospects were more favorable. Aided by Minister

8. See Denby's despatch to Olney in *Foreign Relations* (1897), p. 57.

9. T. Dennett, *Americans in Eastern Asia, a Critical Study of the Policy of the United States with Reference to China, Japan, and Korea in the 19th Century* (New York, 1922), p. 598.

10. Vagts, *Deutschland und die Vereinigten Staaten*, II, 963; Denby's despatch was dated May 10, 1895.

11. B. A. Romanov, *Rossia v Manchzhurii, 1892–1906* (Leningrad, 1928), p. 84; and A. Kantorovich, *Amerika v Bor'be za Kitai* (Moscow, 1935), p. 99.

12. Even before the construction of the Trans-Siberian Railway had been decided upon, Russia in 1890 had shown concern over the activities of another foreigner, an Englishman, interested in building Manchurian railways (Langer, *Diplomacy of Imperialism*, I, 171).

13. J. J. Gapanovich, "Sino-Russian Relations in Manchuria, 1892–1906," *The Chinese Social and Political Science Review, 17* (1933), 293–294. This article is an abstract of Romanov, *Rossia v Manchzhurii*. See also pp. 211–243 of the book.

14. There is reason to believe that Bash may not have dropped his Manchurian venture altogether. In January, 1898, the Russian attaché in Washington reported, erroneously, that the American syndicate had acquired a concession. Russia instructed Cassini "to verify the facts and to make an energetic protest against such a patent infringement of China's obligations" (Kantorovich, *Amerika v Bor'be za Kitai*, p. 101; Romanov, *Rossia v Manchzhurii*, pp. 211–212). The history of this episode is obscure, but at any rate the Development Company did not get a concession in Manchuria. Bash seems to have made still another effort later. In 1899 American engineers were sent to Manchuria, probably by the Development Company. An agent of Count Witte, Russian minister of finance, gave them "friendly" advice to leave, hinting at "various inconveniences" if they refused (Gapanovich, *op. cit.*, p. 299). Again the matter is obscure except for the decisive fact that the company did not get a concession.

Denby [15] Bash persuaded the Chinese to sign on November 1, 1896, a preliminary contract giving construction rights between Peking and Hankow. With the intention of making the contract definitive, Clarence Cary and W. D. Washburn (a director of the Pillsbury-Washburn Flour Company, who may have wished to investigate China as a possible market for flour) [16] at once left for the Far East. On their arrival they met with a disagreeable surprise: China, perhaps because of British pressure,[17] now refused to negotiate further. The two men indignantly appealed to Denby for help; and the minister, who had just received instructions from Secretary Olney to use "all proper methods" for promoting American business interests,[18] did not hesitate to lodge a vigorous protest with the Chinese Foreign Office. The American-China Development Company, he said, was composed of men worth "several hundred millions," and he "had to demand" a speedy conclusion of the contract.[19] Alarmed, it would seem, at Denby's tone, the Chinese retreated. Once again all signs pointed to early settlement; and the American-China Development Company sent engineers to survey the region through which the projected line would pass.[20]

John Sherman replaced Richard Olney as secretary of state in March, 1897, some two months after Denby's protest. The new secretary was an elderly, prudent individual, opposed to strong action and anything smacking of the dramatic, quite different in temperament from the forceful Olney. "If my life is prolonged," he had written some years previously, "I will do all I can to add to the strength and prosperity of the United States, but nothing to extend its limits or to add new dangers by acquisitions of foreign

15. In reporting this success Denby, possibly having in mind Olney's recent instruction to employ "all proper methods" for the extension of American commercial interests in China, mentioned with obvious pride that he had rendered "all possible assistance" to his compatriots (*Foreign Relations* [1897], p. 59, Denby to Olney, February 15, 1897).

16. See C. B. Kuhlmann, *The Development of the Flour-Milling Industry in the United States with Special Reference to the Industry in Minneapolis* (Boston and New York, 1929), pp. 134–135, 152; *Foreign Relations* (1897), p. 58; Denby to Olney, January 10, 1897; Rockhill papers, Wilson to Rockhill, November 25, 1896, and April 27, 1897.

17. *Foreign Relations* (1897), p. 58, Denby to Olney, January 10, 1897.

18. *Ibid.*, p. 56, Olney to Denby, December 19, 1896.

19. *Ibid.*, p. 57, Denby to Olney, January 10, 1897.

20. A. J. Barry, "Railway Development in China," *Journal of the Royal Society of Arts, 57* (1909), 548.

territory." [21] Such a man was sure to interpret strictly Olney's prescription of "all proper methods" for diplomats backing American businesses in China; [22] and unfortunately for Denby the task of answering the minister's report of his protest to the Chinese devolved upon Sherman. The reply amounted to a rebuke. It warned Denby to be more cautious about endorsing business concerns. [23]

A few weeks later the Chinese officials again changed their minds about the Peking-Hankow concession. They signed in May, 1897, a preliminary contract awarding the concession to a Belgian syndicate and in 1898 concluded the definitive contract. [24] Despite all the work of Bash, Cary, and Washburn, the American-China Development Company had failed in central China as well as in Manchuria.

Did Sherman's rebuke to Denby help to cause this second failure? Although the evidence is by no means conclusive, there is some reason to believe that it may have done so. [25] But whatever the explanation the officials of the company were convinced—and this is the significant point—that Secretary Sherman was hopelessly incompetent and was depriving them of the support to which they were so eminently entitled. Angered by the negative attitude in Washington which threatened to undo all their plans, these men, like many exporters of cotton goods, became eager to put all possible pressure on the government in order to force a change in policy.

21. J. Sherman, *Recollections of Forty Years in the House, Senate, and Cabinet, an Autobiography* (2 vols., Chicago and New York, 1895), II, 1216.

22. Sherman's point of view is evident in his reaction to a request for support made by a certain W. von Milchling, agent in China for the Columbia Iron Works and Dry Dock Company of Baltimore. Sherman told Denby to do nothing beyond informing China that von Milchling was the firm's accredited agent (Department of State, Instructions, China, *5*, 506, Sherman to Denby, January 3, 1898).

23. *Foreign Relations* (1897), pp. 59–60, Sherman to Denby, March 8, 1897.

24. For the preliminary contract dated May 10, 1897, see Joseph, *Foreign Diplomacy in China*, p. 179. Langer, *Diplomacy of Imperialism*, II, 679, dates the final contract as June 27, 1898; H. B. Morse, *International Relations of the Chinese Empire* (3 vols., London and New York, 1910–18), III, 87, dates it as June 26, 1898.

25. On this point see S. H. Tan, "The Diplomacy of American Investments in China" (Chicago University, unpublished thesis), p. 498; H. B. Morse, *The Trade and Administration of the Chinese Empire* (London and New York, 1908), p. 86. For another possible explanation of the second failure see *Accounts and Papers, China*, No. 1 (1899), p. 89, where a Chinese official is quoted as declaring that he had originally intended to use American capital but, the conditions named by Cary and Washburn being "too hard," had turned to Belgium, a country of "inconsiderable" strength not dangerous to China.

The indignation of the business interests came to a head in January, 1898. Early in the month, in the midst of the excitement over German and Russian aggression in China, Secretary Sherman granted an interview to the *Philadelphia Press*. He declared flatly that the partition of China was unlikely and that even if it should occur "the powers would gladly seize the opportunity to trade with us. Our commercial interests would not suffer, as far as I can see, in the least—quite the contrary." [26] Backing up the secretary, two other influential public men, Nelson Dingley, chairman of the Ways and Means Committee, and C. K. Davis, chairman of the Senate Committee on Foreign Relations, made similar predictions.[27]

Such observations were little short of anathema to the special business interests. Clarence Cary, back from his unsuccessful mission to the Far East, ridiculed the secretary's "quaint and dangerous" notions; [28] and the *Journal of Commerce* saw yet another proof of Sherman's "serious intellectual limitations." [29] For some of the special interests the secretary's statement seems to have acted as a kind of precipitating factor—the one additional element required for a decision to act. On January 6, 1898, two days after the account of the interview appeared in the *Press*, Clarence Cary, John Foord, and representatives of certain other businesses with Chinese connections met in Cary's office in Wall Street, New York City. James McGee of the Standard Oil Company presided. At the meeting these men set up what they called the Committee on American Interests in China. They gave it the heavy assignment of taking whatever steps might be necessary in order to win the government to a policy of firm support of American business interests in China.[30] The committee's members were Clarence Cary; John Foord; Everett Frazar, head of Frazar and Company, an American trading house with headquarters in Shanghai; S. D. Brewster, partner in Deering, Milliken and Company, exporters of cotton goods to China; and Captain E. L. Zalinski, of the Bethlehem Iron Company—all of them, with the possible exception of Foord, representatives of firms financially involved in China.

---

26. *Philadelphia Press,* January 4, 1898.
27. *Ibid.*
28. C. Cary, "China's Complications and American Trade," *Forum, 25* (1898), 25.
29. *Journal of Commerce and Commercial Bulletin,* January 5, 1898. The *Journal* cited the loss of the cotton market in Madagascar, which, it thought, made Sherman's complacency all the more incomprehensible.
30. *The American Asiatic Association, 1899* (privately printed pamphlet), p. 10.

The Committee on American Interests in China was the first organization formed by American businessmen for the express purpose of effecting a change in Far Eastern policy. Of modest influence at the outset, it developed into a powerful pressure group. Its campaign to "arouse the administration" was of such consequence as to require examination.

V

THE CAMPAIGN UNDER WAY

THE campaign of the Committee on American Interests in China got under way against a background of continuing threats to the integrity of the Chinese Empire. With Germany in firm occupation of Shantung Province the Chinese saw no alternative to making a settlement. They therefore on March 6, 1898, leased to Germany for ninety-nine years a strategic part of Shantung and granted her railway and mining rights in the whole of the province, one of the richest in the empire.[1] France too was active. Already supreme in Hainan, she enlarged her sphere of influence by adding in April, 1898, the provinces bordering on Tongking and shortly afterward the bay of Kwangchow-wan.[2] Japan, not to be outdone by her European mentors, won from China an agreement never to alienate to any third power the wealthy province of Fukien.[3]

Much more serious was the crisis over Port Arthur, which not only threatened to lead to general conflict but also directly affected the American market in north China and Manchuria.[4] The Russian warships which had anchored at Port Arthur in the autumn of 1897 were showing no signs of departure; and the longer they stayed the more worried became other nations, above all Great Britain. To counter Russia the British government in January, 1898, formally expressed its determination to preserve the Open Door, "even . . . if necessary, at the cost of war." Rivalry over a loan to China heightened the Anglo-Russian tension. Although Great Britain emerged triumphant in the loan dispute when China agreed to borrow from the British-owned Hongkong and Shanghai Bank, British elation did not last long. It vanished altogether with news of extensive Russian demands. Russia on March 3 insisted

1. J. V. A. MacMurray, *Treaties and Agreements with and concerning China, 1894–1919* (2 vols., New York, 1921), I, 112–116.
2. *Ibid.*, I, 123, 128–130.
3. *Ibid.*, I, 126.
4. This account is based on Joseph, *Foreign Diplomacy in China,* chaps. x, xi; and Langer, *Diplomacy of Imperialism,* Vol. II, chap. xiv.

that China lease to her the southern tip of the Liaotung Peninsula (including Port Arthur and Talienwan, an important commercial center) and permit her to construct and operate a railway running the length of Manchuria, from the Siberian border down to the leased territory.

Since there was no doubt that these demands menaced and, indeed, almost closed the Open Door in one part of the Chinese Empire, Great Britain now had to decide whether or not to carry out her threat of going to war. But first she turned to Washington. Would the United States, she inquired, with pointed reference to the Russians, cooperate in opposing "action . . . which may tend to restrict freedom of commerce of all nations in China?" [5] America, absorbed by the approaching conflict with Spain, refused to commit herself.[6] Unwilling to fight alone, Great Britain now concluded that Port Arthur after all was not worth a war. Her decision left China with no choice but to yield, and on March 27, 1898, she met the principal Russian demands.[7]

In some respects more disturbing to businessmen than Russian encroachments in Manchuria and certainly far more disturbing than German, French, and Japanese moves in other sections of the Empire were indications that Great Britain might not be so devoted a proponent of the Open Door as she liked to appear. The American business press respected Britain. Along with the United States and Japan she was, its editors believed, a good, constitutional power; on the other hand, Russia, France, and Germany tended to be bad autocracies. But early in 1898 this simple faith suffered a rude shock. Great Britain in February laid claim to much the largest and most valuable sphere of influence yet, the entire Yangtsze Valley. Moreover, in May she leased Kowloon,[8] and in July Weihaiwei.[9] To bewildered Americans it looked very much as though the British might be deserting the cause of righteousness and going the way of the autocracies. Would the Open Door soon have no defender except the United States? In a discouraged mood Minister Denby wrote to Secretary Sherman of

5. A. L. P. Dennis, *Adventures in American Diplomacy, 1896–1906* (New York, E. P. Dutton & Co., 1928), pp. 170–171.

6. *Ibid.* The United States refused despite Minister Denby's suggestion, March 19, that England, "with our moral support," might yet call a halt to Russia's progress in Manchuria and so "save our treaty rights in that country" (Department of State, Despatches, China, *103*, No. 2889, Denby to Sherman, March 19, 1898).

7. MacMurray, *Treaties and Agreements*, I, 119–121.

8. *Ibid.*, I, 130–131.

9. *Ibid.*, I, 152–153.

his fear of the coming breakup of the Chinese Empire: England would take the Yangtsze Valley; France, the southern provinces; Russia, Manchuria; and Germany, Shantung. "The greatest market of the world . . ." Denby lamented, "will be lost to us." [10]

Against this background of threatening partition and also, it will be recalled, against the background of indifference in Washington epitomized by Sherman's indiscreet statement to the *Philadelphia Press*, the Committee on American Interests in China began its campaign to transform Far Eastern policy. It prepared a petition in January, persuaded sixty-eight firms (many of them exporters of cotton goods) [11] to sign it, and sent copies to the chambers of commerce of New York, Boston, San Francisco, and Cleveland, and to the Philadelphia Board of Trade. The petition urged these widespread organizations to draw up resolutions demanding of the government that the country's "important commercial interests" in China be "duly and promptly . . . safeguarded." [12]

As a direct consequence of the petition all these chambers except that of Cleveland [13] adopted and forwarded to Washington statements along the suggested lines. In addition, commercial organizations in Baltimore [14] and Seattle [15] took similar action. (Since the resolutions from these last two cities contained phrasing almost identical with that of the New York chamber it is evident that they too resulted from the committee's petition.) Furthermore a number of businessmen in China, representing most of the Ameri-

10. Department of State, Despatches, China, *103*, No. 2867, Denby to Sherman, February 14, 1898.

11. Among those signing the petition were Frazar and Co., the American Trading Co., Fearon, Daniel and Co. (all three American firms in China); the Standard Oil Co.; Bliss, Fabyan and Co. (the company of C. N. Bliss, secretary of the interior, which was agent for several New England cotton mills); Catlin and Co. (agent for a great many southern mills); Smith, Hogg and Gardner, Deering, Milliken and Co., Minot, Hooper and Co., Wheelwright, Eldredge and Co., Woodward, Baldwin and Co. (all five exporters to China of cotton goods); the Baldwin Locomotive Works; the Rogers Locomotive Co.; the Brooks Locomotive Works; the Illinois Steel Co.; the Carnegie Steel Co.; the Bethlehem Iron Co.; and the Westinghouse Electric and Manufacturing Co.

12. *The American Asiatic Association, 1899,* pp. 10–11; New York Chamber of Commerce, *Annual Report* (1897–98), p. 74.

13. Perhaps because it had fewer business connections with China than the other cities, the Cleveland chamber did not send a resolution.

14. Department of State, Miscellaneous Letters, March, 1898, Part 2, Baltimore Chamber of Commerce to Sherman, March 17, 1898.

15. *Ibid.,* April, 1898, Part 2, Seattle Chamber of Commerce to McKinley, April 14, 1898.

can firms in that country,[16] informed the New York chamber that they strongly approved its resolution and were convinced of the urgent need, in order to protect American interests against Russia, of "immediate action" in the Far East.[17] And finally, an influential British organization, the British China Association, expressed similar approval.[18] The New York chamber promptly forwarded both these communications to Washington.

The resolution of the New York Chamber of Commerce, sent to the State Department on February 3, 1898, served as a model for most of the others and created the greatest impression in the capital and throughout the country. It contended:

That the trade of the United States to China is now rapidly increasing, and is destined, with the further opening of that country, to assume large proportions unless arbitrarily debarred by the action of foreign governments. . . . That, in view of the changes threatening to future trade development of the United States in China, the Chamber of Commerce . . . respectfully and earnestly urge that such proper steps be taken as will commend themselves to your wisdom for the prompt and energetic defence of the existing treaty rights of our citizens in China, and for the preservation and protection of their important commercial interests in that Empire.[19]

The other resolutions argued in similar vein. The Philadelphia Board of Trade (February 25, 1898) asserted that the United States should act forthwith in order to preserve "all the privileges enjoyed under existing treaty rights";[20] the San Francisco chamber (March 8) asked the government to "maintain and promote . . . commercial rights" in China;[21] and the Boston chamber (March 30) stated: the "rapidly growing trade with . . . China is so important, that we cannot refrain from . . .

16. For a complete list see *ibid.,* New York Chamber of Commerce to Sherman, April 16, 1898.

17. *Ibid.,* March, 1898, Part 2, New York Chamber of Commerce to Day, March 16, 1898.

18. *Ibid.*

19. *Ibid.,* February, 1898, Part 1, New York Chamber of Commerce to McKinley, February 3, 1898. Also New York Chamber of Commerce, *Annual Report* (1897–98), p. 75.

20. Department of State, Miscellaneous Letters, February, 1898, Part 3, Philadelphia Board of Trade to McKinley, February 25, 1898. The State Department, to which the communication was referred, replied that the matter was having full attention (*idem,* Domestic Letters, *226,* 169, Day to Fraley, March 3, 1898).

21. *Idem,* Miscellaneous Letters, March, 1898, Part 2, San Francisco Chamber of Commerce to McKinley, March 8, 1898.

expressing the hope that . . . the fullest protection will be accorded to United States commercial interests in that country." [22]

Thus the Committee on American Interests within some four months of its formation had been directly responsible for eight communications urging the government to defend the country's rights in China. In addition there were during the same period two resolutions which the committee inspired only in the sense that it had set the example for others to follow. The first was adopted by the China and Japan Trading Company, exporters of cotton goods to the Far East. Warned by its Shanghai branch of a "critical" situation requiring "immediate action," the company on March 16, 1898, wrote to Cornelius N. Bliss, secretary of the interior, and partner in Bliss, Fabyan and Company, another exporter of cottons to China. The Trading Company noted the grave threat hanging over the American cotton-goods industry as a result of Russian "aggression" and begged the government to give immediate and "forceful expression of its intentions to have equal freedom for trade in China." [23] The second resolution was adopted about a month later; in it the New England Shoe and Leather Association, addressing President McKinley, recommended in strong terms Anglo-American cooperation to preserve equal commercial opportunities in China.[24]

Undoubtedly these ten resolutions made themselves felt. A qualified observer, John Foord, went so far as to maintain that because of them "the whole subject of American interests in the Far East began to assume a position of national prominence." [25] All the resolutions and especially that of the New York chamber attracted widespread attention.[26] Extensive comments in leading newspapers throughout the nation were to the effect that they were "notable," [27] "timely," [28] proof that "business men have not misunder-

22. *Ibid.*, Boston Chamber of Commerce to McKinley, March 30, 1898.

23. *Ibid.*, China and Japan Trading Company to Bliss, March 16, 1898.

24. *Idem*, Domestic Letters, *227*, 474–475. The resolution was dated April 17, 1898. Since few Chinese used the western type of shoe it is not clear why this association concerned itself with China. Perhaps like many Americans it was looking ahead to the potential market.

25. J. Foord, "The Genesis of the Open Door," *Asia; Journal of the American Asiatic Association, 2* (1902), 122.

26. The New York chamber has a large collection of press clippings relating to its resolution.

27. *Journal of Commerce and Commercial Bulletin,* January 31, 1898. This issue was published prior to the adoption of the petition by the chamber (February 3), but there is no discrepancy since the petition was made public on January 28.

28. *Erie Herald* (Erie, Pennsylvania), February 3, 1898.

stood the situation," [29] worthy of being "sustained by the commercial organizations of the entire country," [30] and failed only in not recognizing explicitly that Great Britain was fighting the American battle.[31] Moreover, the resolutions stirred Secretary Sherman to an unusual degree of action. He assured the New York chamber on February 11, 1898, of his "most careful consideration" of Chinese affairs.[32] On the same day he instructed Ambassador White at Berlin to warn Germany that the United States, as a power having substantial commercial relations with China, was "naturally" concerned over the occupation of Kiaochao.[33] And about a month later he directed Ambassador Hitchcock at St. Petersburg to inquire into Russia's intentions at Port Arthur. The United States, the secretary said, favored "open trade" with China.[34]

The Far Eastern situation, as it happened, continued still further to deteriorate. But the Committee on American Interests must have felt encouraged by Sherman's reaction. The administration had moved at least a little distance in what many businessmen considered the right direction. Having tasted some success the committee had every reason to continue its efforts. Yet at this very moment, just when the prospect seemed somewhat brighter, an event occurred which for a time interrupted the campaign of the special business interests. In April, 1898, the United States went to war against Spain.

29. *Commercial and Financial Chronicle, 66* (1898), 312.

30. *Times* (Philadelphia), February 2, 1898.

31. *New York Times,* February 5, 1898.

32. Department of State, Domestic Letters, *225*, 386–387, Sherman to Orr, February 11, 1898.

33. *Idem,* Instructions, Germany, *20*, 371–373, Sherman to White, February 11, 1898. Much of this instruction has wording identical with that of Sherman's reply to the New York chamber.

34. *Ibid.,* Russia, *18*, Sherman to Hitchcock, March 16, 1898.

VI

WARTIME INTERLUDE

THE Spanish-American War affected the campaign of the business interests in various ways. On the one hand it so absorbed the country's attention that the flow of inspired memorials on the situation in China which had characterized the first months of 1898 came to an abrupt end. But in other ways it furthered the efforts of the Committee on American Interests in China, and its net effect was certainly to strengthen the forces working for a strong policy in that crumbling empire.

One favorable development was the departure of John Sherman from the State Department. A week after hostilities commenced William R. Day succeeded him as secretary of state. Day soon demonstrated in the eyes of the special business interests the superiority of his Far Eastern policy. Hardly two months in office, the new secretary recommended to Congress that a special commission be sent to China to study means of increasing American exports; he cited as proof of widespread desire to trade with that country the memorial of February, 1898, from the New York Chamber of Commerce. Denying, in effect, Sherman's dictum that partition would not affect America adversely, Day asserted flatly: "The United States has important interests at stake in the partition of commercial facilities in regions which are likely to offer developing markets for its goods." [1] Although it did not point to such sweeping changes in policy as many businessmen favored, Day's recommendation nonetheless indicated a more sympathetic attitude toward American interests in China than the administration had shown in recent years. To the *Journal of Commerce*, despite the failure of Congress to set up a commission, the changed atmosphere in Washington seemed "remarkable." [2]

But however great an improvement over his predecessor, the new secretary of state still left much to be desired by the business

1. *House Document*, No. 536, 55th Congress, Second Session. Day's recommendation was dated June 9, 1898.
2. *Journal of Commerce and Commercial Bulletin*, June 18, 1898.

interests. The officials of the American-China Development Company in particular had reason for dissatisfaction because on two occasions Day rejected their requests. Just before the war started the Development Company finally got a concession: it signed with the Chinese on April 14, 1898, a contract giving construction rights for a railway between Hankow and Canton. Feeling the need of official support the company then asked Secretary Day for protection against possible "prejudice from foreign . . . interference." [3] Day refused. The department, he said, preferred not to commit itself to future action before a clear need should arise.[4] Despite this rebuff the company went ahead with its plans, and soon a survey party began to map out the route of the projected railway. General William Barclay Parsons, a well-known engineer, headed the mission; and Charles Denby, Jr., son of the minister, served as interpreter and manager.[5]

During the war the American-China Development Company established close relations with a British syndicate which likewise aspired to build railways in China.[6] This was the British and Chinese Corporation, a concern that numbered among its members some of the most prominent individuals and firms in Great Britain: the Hongkong and Shanghai Banking Corporation; Jardine, Matheson and Company; Anthony Gibbs and Company; Sir John Wolf Barry; Sir Thomas Sutherland; Cosmo Bonsor; the Barings; and Hambro, Sassoon, and Rothschild interests.[7] The American and British groups realized that they might benefit by working together in China and began to seek a basis for cooperation. Somewhat unexpectedly, far-reaching prospects opened up; and in short order the negotiators drew up a preliminary agreement whereby each company was to offer the other one-half interest in any business subsequently obtained by either in China.[8] But

3. Department of State, Miscellaneous Letters, May, 1898, Part 1, Bash to Day, May 3, 1898.
4. *Ibid.,* August, 1898, Part 2, Day to Bash, May 13, 1898 (copy).
5. W. B. Parsons, *An American Engineer in China* (New York, 1900), gives an interesting account of the experiences of the survey party.
6. Calvin Brice, the company's president, got in touch in London with the British syndicate (Department of State, Miscellaneous Letters, August, 1898, Part 2, Cary and Whitridge to Day, August 19, 1898).
7. For the complete list of members see *ibid.*
8. In the new contract the Development Company obligated itself to provide at least $20,000,000, and more if necessary, for constructing the railway. Later estimates showed the need to raise this figure to the substantial sum of $40,000,000. The British and Chinese Corporation offered to provide not only the additional $20,000,000 but, if desirable, almost the entire $40,000,000. On this matter see W. W.

before finally concluding the matter the British asked the Americans to get from the United States government a "certain assurance," similar to a guarantee from the Foreign Office which they, the British, were enjoying. Accordingly the attorneys for the Development Company, Cary and Whitridge, the firm of Clarence Cary, requested the State Department to agree to uphold the railway contract as a "binding engagement upon the imperial Chinese Government." [9] For the second time Secretary Day turned the company down: The government, he said, "has always declined to become the guarantors of . . . contracts with foreign governments." [10] Although Cary and Whitridge refused to accept this rebuff as final and seem to have conferred a few days later with the president and the secretary of state, still they did not get a guarantee.[11] Fortunately for the Development Company the British decided not to insist on the "certain assurance"; and the two companies on February 1, 1899, made their agreement definitive.[12]

Thus the American-China Development Company, although it had failed with Secretary Day, succeeded during the war with Spain in strengthening itself and thereby in improving its prospects for final success. It was not long, as will appear, before the big-business administration of McKinley, perhaps impressed by such a potent combination of Anglo-American capital, was for the first time giving strong diplomatic support to the American railway venture.

Far more significant than Day's replacement of Sherman, more significant even than the achievements of the Development Company, was another wartime occurrence: the occupation of the Philippine Islands. Admiral Dewey's famous victory at Manila

Rockhill, *Treaties and Conventions with or concerning China and Korea, 1894–1904, together with Various State Papers and Documents Affecting Foreign Interests* (Washington, 1904), p. 252; A. J. Barry, "Railway Development in China," *Journal of the Royal Society of Arts, 57* (1909), 549–550; Department of State, Miscellaneous Letters, August, 1898, Part 2, Cary and Whitridge to Day, August 19, 1898.

9. Department of State, Miscellaneous Letters, August, 1898, Part 2, Cary and Whitridge to Day, August 19, 1898.

10. *Idem,* Domestic Letters, *231,* 88–89, Day to Cary and Whitridge, August 24, 1898.

11. *Idem,* Miscellaneous Letters, August, 1898, Part 3, Cary and Whitridge to Day, August 30, 1898.

12. *Accounts and Papers, China,* No. 1 (1899), pp. 325–326; Rockhill, *Treaties and Conventions,* pp. 345–347.

Bay on May 1, 1898, directed attention to a part of the world of which Americans had previously been almost entirely unaware. As time passed the country became more and more conscious of the Far East: first, because of the prolonged, bitter controversy as to whether or not to annex the Philippines; and second, because once annexation had been decided upon the United States, suddenly become a Far Eastern power, found itself deeply involved in the power politics of eastern Asia. A thorough reconsideration of policy toward China became imperative; for more convincingly than the most plausible arguments the new American position in the Pacific persuaded governmental official and ordinary citizen alike that the fate of the Chinese did indeed concern the United States.

But annexation of the Philippine Islands, it is essential to note, did not lead in any mechanical, inevitable sense to the Open Door Policy. Most Americans needed help to grasp the connection between occupation of that archipelago and intervention in China. (Here was an opportunity of which the special business interests took advantage.) Moreover, the acquisition of the Philippines, although a cause of greater attention to China, was itself in some measure the result of already existent interest in that country; [13] and at least some of this interest must be attributed to the campaign of the business groups. In other words, annexation of the islands did most certainly hasten the adoption of the Open Door Policy; but annexation in its turn was partly the result of business pressure.

One other event of marked significance occurred during the war. Chiefly under the inspiration of John Foord [14] the Committee on American Interests in China had realized for some time that it was too loose and informal a body for maximum effectiveness. A more elaborate organization, the British China Association, already operated in Great Britain; and the committee believed that Americans would benefit from a similar American body. Accordingly on June 9, 1898, the committee dissolved itself and established a new organization which took the name American Asiatic Association.

13. People often argued that since most of the great powers were acquiring bases in the Orient the United States would be foolish not to take advantage of what seemed a providential opportunity for securing its own interests in that part of the world. Take the Philippines in order to protect the Chinese market—this was a frequently advanced proposition.

14. *New York Times,* April 19, 1922.

The association set up headquarters in New York and branches in Shanghai, Tokyo, and Kobe.[15] All the members of the Committee on American Interests joined the new organization. Four of them held key posts: Everett Frazar became the Association's president, S. D. Brewster vice-president, John Foord secretary, and Clarence Cary a member of the executive committee.[16]

The strategic position of the last two men is remarkable. As secretary of the American Asiatic Association, editor of the *Journal of Commerce*, and editor of *Asia*, a periodical started by the association, John Foord had opportunities for influencing Far Eastern policy which few, if any, outside the government could equal. In fact not many governmental officials had as much influence as Foord. Clarence Cary too, as counsel for the American-China Development Company and member of the executive committee of the Asiatic Association, was strongly placed for shaping opinion and policy.

With a full-time staff and permanent officers the American Asiatic Association became a considerably more effective pressure group than the Committee on American Interests in China had been. Like the committee, the association strove to bring the country's policy toward China into line with its own interests.[17] ". . . *what American and British merchants require,*" wrote the associations's president, "*for the maintenance of their trade with China are open ports,* under their treaties, *without any outside restrictions or interference.* It is in this direction that we have to devote our energies as occasions arise, and in conference with our [New York] Chamber of Commerce, the State Department at Washington and with the Chambers in the principal ports in the East." [18]

Within a few days of its establishment the association had forty-eight members, for the most part the same individuals and firms

15. Minute-Book of the American Asiatic Association (1898–1919), p. 8; and *The American Asiatic Association, 1899*, p. 22.

16. *The American Asiatic Association, 1899*, p. 2.

17. C. Beresford, *The Break-Up of. China* (New York and London, 1899), p. 437; the American Asiatic Association "watches over the American commercial interests in the Far East, and brings political pressure to bear in furtherance of those interests."

18. *Asia; Journal of the American Asiatic Association, 1* (1898), 14; speech of October 31, 1898; italics original. The association's constitution stated as one of its purposes: "To secure the advantage of sustained watchfulness and readiness for action, attainable by union and permanent organization, in respect of . . . Asiatic trade, as well as in matters of legislation, or treaties affecting the same" (*ibid., 1* [1899], 45).

that had signed the petition drawn up in January, 1898, by the Committee on American Interests in China: namely, American firms with offices in Shanghai, New York agents for the cotton interests, and iron and steel manufacturers.[19] By the end of 1900 there were 242 members, among the more prominent of whom were Calvin Brice and W. D. Washburn, officials of the American-China Development Company; W. W. Rockhill, who drafted the Open Door notes of 1899; [20] Seth Low, soon to be mayor of New York City; the General Electric Company, the Great Northern Railroad Company, the Pacific Cable Company of New York, the Guaranty Trust Company, the Maryland Steel Company, the New York Central and Hudson River Railroad Company, the Diamond Match Company, the Equitable Life Assurance Society of the United States, the Mutual Life Insurance Company of New York, the Mercantile Trust Company, the Newport News Shipbuilding and Dry Dock Company, the Pepperell Manufacturing Company, some Pacific coast shipping companies, and various southern cotton mills.[21]

The association had three honorary members: Charles Denby, former minister to China; Morris K. Jesup, president of the New York Chamber of Commerce; and John Barrett, minister-resident to Siam from 1894 to 1898. The last named is particularly noteworthy. An enthusiastic and persistent advocate of America's mission in the Pacific, Barrett had influence which seems to have been comparable to Clarence Cary's although less than John Foord's. "For five years," he said in 1899, "I have hammered away in reports to the Government, letters to Chambers of Commerce, and contributions to newspapers, magazines, and reviews . . . with the hope of thus awakening our Government, as well as our manufacturers and exporters, to an appreciation of the splendid field [in the Far East and especially in China] awaiting their best efforts." [22]

19. See p. 34.
20. Rockhill joined the association in October, 1899, just after the notes of September 6, 1899, were sent but was in touch with it before then (Rockhill papers, Rockhill to Foord, August 18, 1899).
21. *The American Asiatic Association, 1900*, pp. 27–32. For a list of all the other members as of November 14, 1900, see the Appendix below.
22. *North American Review, 169* (1899), 166–167. In a letter to the author Mr. Barrett wrote:
"I never delivered any addresses under the auspices of any organization or of any backing that had any 'axe to grind,' so to speak. I was not hired by any government or organization to be a protagonist of any cause. In accepting all kinds of

The association, as soon as it came into being, forwarded to the secretary of state its membership list which, it boasted, included "many of the chief firms, corporations, and individuals" doing business with China.[23] It was quick also to get in touch with the *Journal of Commerce*, to which it expressed a "sense of obligation" for "efforts in promoting their common purpose." [24] Desiring to reach the country at large as well as the government, the association soon began to publish the periodical *Asia; Journal of the American Asiatic Association* under John Foord's editorship. The magazine appeared at regular fortnightly intervals, spreading the gospel of the vital necessity for a policy that would ensure equality of treatment for American commerce with China.

As a result of the formation of an effective pressure group and also of greater general appreciation of America's stake in the Chinese Empire, businessmen concerned about the fate of that empire emerged from the Spanish-American War in a considerably stronger position for influencing foreign policy. Even by the autumn of 1898, when the American Asiatic Association had existed only a few months, it had already, in the opinion of the *Journal of Commerce*, "exercised a salutary influence in educating public sentiment" and had "been one of the agencies which have impelled our Government to adopt a more vigorous policy in China." [25] The future looked auspicious for the special business interests when, after a few months of conflict, an armistice in the autumn of 1898 brought hostilities to a close.

---

invitations from chambers of commerce, universities, various cultural and civic organizations, etc., I always emphasized that I represented no special interest and was arguing no cause except that of the welfare of the United States and of the countries with which it had good relations.

"Perhaps the fact that everyone realized that I was not speaking in behalf of any special interest except that of my country was a powerful factor in attention being given to what I said. Between the time I returned from Asia in early 1899 and the time of my departure on the 1902–3 tour [as special envoy of President Roosevelt and commissioner general of the St. Louis Exposition] I was overwhelmed with invitations from all classes of groups and organizations to discuss with them . . . Oriental . . . questions."

The career of Charles Denby, Jr., was somewhat similar. Like Barrett Denby resigned from the diplomatic service and devoted himself to propaganda for a strong policy in the Far East.

23. Department of State, Miscellaneous Letters, June, 1898, Part 2, Frazar to Day, June 17, 1898. For Day's reply see *idem*, Domestic Letters, *229*, 509, Day to Frazar, June 23, 1898.

24. Minute-Book of the American Asiatic Association (1898–1919), p. 1, meeting of June 21, 1898.

25. *Journal of Commerce and Commercial Bulletin,* October 21, 1898.

VII

CRISIS

WITH the armistice of August 12, 1898, the war with Spain came virtually to an end. Once again the special business interests carried on their campaign without wartime distractions. The need for renewed propaganda was all too evident. As the blindest could see, the situation in China was heading toward a crisis. Despite the new American position in the Far East following upon conquest of the Philippines, the forces making for partition appeared to be gaining strength.

Almost coincidentally with the armistice, news from London added to the apprehension which had arisen earlier in the year over British expansion in China.[1] Addressing the House of Commons Arthur Balfour, acting foreign minister, said with reference to China: "A concession must be given to someone, and when the someone has got it, other people must be excluded. . . . That is not inequality of treatment." [2] And a little later Joseph Chamberlain, the colonial secretary, was equally ominous: it was not to England's interest, he said, "to give anything like a guarantee of the integrity and independence of an empire which appeared to be decaying." [3] It was hard to reconcile such apparent acceptance of discrimination, such apparent complacency over the integrity and even independence of the Chinese Empire, with earlier British devotion to the Open Door. And if Great Britain should throw in her weight for partition the prospect indeed would be grim. The *United States Investor* reflected the general pessimism:

Now the people of the United States are just awaking to the fact that we are capable of occupying a dominant position in the commerce of Asia. But almost as this consciousness takes possession of us comes the announcement that the door is about to be closed, and that soon will ring the cry, "Too late, too late, ye cannot enter now." We say with a full conviction of the seriousness of our words, that no policy,

1. See p. 33.
2. Langer, *Diplomacy of Imperialism*, II, 681.
3. *Ibid.*, II, 681–682.

however drastic, which our Government finds it necessary to pursue in order to guarantee equal trade rights to everybody in China, should be neglected.[4]

In the gathering gloom one bright spot stood out: the McKinley administration had quite forsaken the detached attitude toward the fate of China which had characterized it during the tenure of John Sherman. ". . . it will be my aim," said President McKinley in his annual message to Congress at the end of 1898, "to subserve our large interests in that quarter [China] by all means appropriate to the constant policy of our Government."[5] A considerable distance separates this vigorous assertion from Sherman's unconcerned pronouncement to the *Philadelphia Press* the preceding January. "The remarkable thing," the Boston *Transcript* observed, "the revelation of the message, is the extent to which China has come into calculations at Washington."[6] The change, of course, vastly encouraged the business interests, which took part of the credit to themselves. ". . . the new attitude," the *Journal of Commerce* asserted flatly, ". . . is partly the result of the American Asiatic Association."[7]

About a month after the armistice McKinley appointed John Hay, then ambassador to Great Britain, to succeed William Day as secretary of state. To the business interests Day had been an improvement on Sherman; and Hay, a firm believer in commercial equality in China,[8] was an improvement on Day. In fact John Hay came close to being their ideal secretary of state.

The new secretary soon had ample opportunity to put into practice his ideas on Far Eastern policy. The day he took office crowds of unruly Chinese in Peking jostled and badly frightened several foreigners. The Boxer uprising was less than a year away;

4. *United States Investor, 9* (1898), 1177. See also *Literary Digest, 17* (1898), 273, which contains many quotations, almost all of them reflecting pessimism about China. But *Iron Age, 62* (1898), 17, has a more optimistic view.

5. *Foreign Relations* (1898), p. lxxii.

6. *Literary Digest, 17* (1898), 710.

7. *Journal of Commerce and Commercial Bulletin,* January 24, 1899.

8. People suspected that Hay's position in this matter partly explained his appointment. Said the *Providence Journal:* "It is barely possible that the president has selected him [Hay] on the most general grounds, but it is not likely. . . . England stands for the commercial policy that would be most beneficial to us, and just as the war clouds are lowering on the oriental horizon, Mr. McKinley calls to his assistance one of our most distinguished advocates of Anglo-American friendliness (*Public Opinion, 25* [1898], 232). See *ibid.,* p. 233, for a similar citation from the Baltimore *News.*

ominous rumors already were prevalent; the future hung heavy
with anxiety. Hay resolved upon firm measures. He sent two gunboats from Manila to Taku, the port most accessible to Peking,
and telegraphed Minister Edwin Conger, Denby's successor, to
"act vigorously for the protection of Americans." [9] Here at last
was the kind of action dear to the special business interests.
Promptly and unanimously the New York Chamber of Commerce
adopted a resolution expressing to Hay its "high appreciation." [10]
The chamber had good reason to be appreciative, for the riots soon
ended and once again the customary calm prevailed.

Disorders in north China and Manchuria threatened to play
into the hands of Russia. Recognizing the danger, some fifty-three
manufacturers and exporters of cotton textiles (among whom were
the Pepperell Manufacturing Company; Bliss, Fabyan and Company; Deering, Milliken and Company; and most of the other
cotton firms, both northern and southern, which have been mentioned in these pages) [11] addressed a noteworthy petition to the
State Department. They pointed out that well over half of all
American exports of cotton goods went to areas in China occupied
or threatened by Russia, and declared that

unless a vigorous policy is pursued on the part of the United States
Government, these markets will be eventually closed to our trade, as
has recently been the case in Madagascar. . . . We earnestly call attention to the above facts, and ask that our representatives at St.
Petersburgh [*sic*] be instructed to give special attention to the subject.[12]

Hay did exactly as requested: he sent one copy of the petition to
Minister Conger and another to H. H. D. Peirce, *chargé d'affaires*
at St. Petersburg; he told both diplomats that "the high character and standing of the signers warrant my calling . . . serious
attention to the subject." [13] Apparently believing further
prodding of Russia necessary, Hay wrote again to Peirce: "You
will be expected to use every opportunity to act energetically in

9. *Foreign Relations* (1898), p. 228, Hay to Conger, October 3, 1898.

10. Department of State, Miscellaneous Letters, October, 1898, Part 1, New York
Chamber of Commerce to Hay, October 10, 1898; New York Chamber of Commerce,
Annual Report (1898–99), p. 46.

11. For a complete list see Department of State, Miscellaneous Letters, January,
1899, Part 1, to Hay, January 3, 1899.

12. *Ibid.*

13. *Idem,* Instructions, Russia, *18,* 156, Hay to Peirce, February 2, 1899; *ibid.*,
China, *5,* 644, Hay to Conger, February 2, 1899.

the sense desired by the numerous and influential signers of the petition." [14] Here was a secretary of state after the heart of the most eager enterprisers in China!

Fresh cause for anxiety came in December, 1898, with reports of pressure by France for a larger concession in Shanghai. Although the French appear to have had some justification for their demand,[15] the news caused the American press to give vent to angry denunciations. One paper labeled France the "ally of barbarism." [16] Instructed by Hay,[17] Conger warned the Chinese not to yield.[18] Again business interests were pleased. The New York Chamber of Commerce adopted another unanimous resolution commending the government,[19] and the American Asiatic Association urged the use of "all available means . . . towards preserving . . . an 'open door.' " [20]

Despite the forthright American stand the United States had itself been doing about the same thing as France: it had been pressing China to enlarge the International Settlement, the name given to the combined British and American concessions in Shanghai.[21] When negotiations collapsed in the spring of 1899 many businessmen in Shanghai were dismayed. Following consultation with the British China Association the American Association of China appealed to its parent organization, the Asiatic Association, for help. The New York body, more than willing to assist,

14. *Ibid., Russia, 18*, 171–172, Hay to Tower, March 10, 1899; *idem, Despatches, China, 106*, No. 162, Conger to Hay, March 15, 1899; *idem*, Instructions, Russia, *18*, 190, Hay to Tower, April 27, 1899.

15. Rockhill papers, Rockhill to Adee, August 24, 1899: "There is no doubt . . . that the French concession is cramped and requires to be extended, and I can conceive of no valid reason for opposing France in securing such extension."

16. *Journal of Commerce and Commercial Bulletin,* January 4, 1899. See also *ibid.,* January 3, 1899, for a report of concern felt by New York merchants.

17. *Foreign Relations* (1899), p. 144.

18. *Ibid.* (1899), pp. 144, 279–283. In subsequent communications to Washington Conger minimized the importance of the incident.

19. Department of State, Miscellaneous Letters, January, 1899, Part 1, New York Chamber of Commerce to Hay, January 7, 1899; New York Chamber of Commerce, *Annual Report* (1898–99), p. 87.

20. Department of State, Miscellaneous Letters, January, 1899, Part 1, Foord to Hay, January 7, 1899. See *ibid.,* December, 1898, Part 4, which has a letter from Frazar to Hay, dated December 31, 1898, stating that the New York chamber and the Asiatic Association were each to meet on January 5 and that they would support the government's protest. The letter said that Frazar was to address both meetings and asked for material on the French concession to be used in his speeches.

21. The United States protested also against a Japanese move to enlarge their concession in Amoy, one of the leading cities in Fukien Province (*Foreign Relations* [1899], p. 151); but the Japanese were successful.

promptly wrote to Hay urging "vigorous action." [22] Hay in turn
sent a copy of the letter to Conger and instructed him to insist on
compliance with the American demand.[23] Not long afterward China
gave in.

Riots in Peking, fears of Russian aggression, and difficulties
with France and China—all these were as nothing compared with
a convergence of incidents in March and April, 1899, which seemed
to bring very near the breakup of the Chinese Empire. The first
signs of danger appeared in Shantung. Germany in March resolved to put an end to various hostile acts which disgruntled
Chinese for several months had been committing in that province.
Accordingly she sent a military expedition into the interior; it
quickly restored law and order. Although of too short duration
to attract much attention the episode was an unpleasant reminder
of the precarious nature of a market about which more and more
Americans were becoming decidedly uneasy. "We must have the
market," said Senator Frye at the time, "or we shall have revolution." [24]

Far more disquieting were other springtime developments.
While German troops were marching through Shantung Italy presented demands for a naval base at San Mun Bay near Shanghai.
The demands alone were bad enough, for Shanghai was much the
most important Chinese port; but they seemed far worse because
of an assertion by the Italian minister of foreign affairs that the
major countries of Europe, including Great Britain, were sup-
porting Italy. Once again the old specter of a concerted plan for
the dismemberment of China raised its head; once again the latent
distrust of the British flared brightly.

The San Mun Bay affair caused considerable trepidation in
American business circles. "A momentous crisis in America's great
interests in the Pacific is now impending," warned the *Journal of
Commerce*, extremely agitated.[25] Although less dramatic, Secretary Hay likewise took the matter seriously. In the midst of the
excitement he wrote to Paul Dana,[26] editor of the New York *Sun:*

22. Department of State, Miscellaneous Letters, March, 1899, Part 2, Foord and
Brewster to Hay, March 23, 1899. This letter was written about two months after
the association denounced the French request for a larger concession.
23. *Idem,* Instructions, China, *5,* 660–661, Hay to Conger, April 3, 1899. See also
idem, Domestic Letters, *236,* 108–109, Hay to Brewster, April 3, 1899.
24. *Journal of Commerce and Commercial Bulletin,* March 21, 1899.
25. *Ibid.,* March 7, 1899.
26. Hay wrote to the chargé d'affaires, H. H. D. Peirce, at St. Petersburg in-

We are, of course, opposed to the dismemberment of that Empire [China], and we do not think that the public opinion of the United States would justify this Government in taking part in the great game of spoliation now going on. At the same time we are keenly alive to the importance of safeguarding our great commercial interests in that Empire and representatives there have orders to watch closely everything that may seem calculated to injure us, and to prevent it by energetic and timely representations. We declined to support the demand of Italy for a lodgment.[27]

As for the American Asiatic Association, so alarming did it consider the new turn of events that it sent its secretary, John Foord, to Washington to confer urgently with various officials. Foord's trip convinced him of the need to modify the association's propaganda, and on his return to New York he won his colleagues to his own point of view.[28] The administration, he contended, was now reliable; the time had come to devote more time and money to "education of the people, the press, and the politicians." [29] To this end the association began to collect a special fund. It used the money, largely contributed by exporters of cotton goods,[30] to expand its propaganda throughout the nation.[31] Although the association did not neglect the government, it increasingly turned its assiduous attention to the general public.

In its "education" of the public the Asiatic Association received valuable assistance from Lord Charles Beresford, former admiral in Her Majesty's Navy and member of Parliament. Representing the Associated Chambers of Commerce of Great Britain, the admiral had recently come to the United States after a tour of China. Beresford was an enthusiastic advocate of Anglo-American cooperation to protect the Open Door; and during the two and a half weeks which elapsed between his arrival in San Francisco

structing him "to act energetically" (see p. 47) just a few days before writing to Dana.

27. Hay to Dana, March 16, 1899; cited in W. R. Thayer, *The Life and Letters of John Hay* (2 vols., Boston and New York, 1915), II, 241.

28. Minute-Book of the American Asiatic Association (1898–1919), p. 17, meeting of March 2, 1899; *ibid.*, p. 19, meeting of March 17, 1899.

29. *Journal of Commerce and Commercial Bulletin*, March 18, 1899. The words quoted were probably written by John Foord.

30. Contributions to the fund were constantly being made. For a complete list of contributors with the amount contributed by each see *Asia; Journal of the American Asiatic Association, 1* (1899), 58, and *1* (1900), 108.

31. Minute-Book of the American Asiatic Association (1898–1919), p. 21, meeting of April 11, 1899; *The American Asiatic Association, 1900*, p. 19.

and his departure from New York in February, 1899,[32] the noble lord hammered home his favorite thesis in a strenuous series of speeches to business organizations in San Francisco, Chicago, Buffalo, and New York. Everywhere he met a cordial reception. Beresford's major speeches were given in New York. There, in consequence of a petition signed by Clarence Cary and Everett Frazar, among others, he addressed the Chamber of Commerce.[33] There too he spoke to the American Asiatic Association at a dinner for which about a hundred prominent citizens paid $20 each.[34] Just before leaving the country Beresford was the guest of honor at a banquet in Washington given by Secretary Hay.

The press regarded the spectacular Englishman with mixed feelings.[35] Many writers supported his arguments; on the other hand not a few, reflecting the traditional distrust of Great Britain, considered him a sinister agent bent on hoodwinking gullible Uncle Sam. But there can be no doubt that Beresford made a deep impression upon numerous businessmen. His speeches, the *Journal of Commerce* reported, contributed greatly to the "education of the mercantile community." [36] When the energetic admiral sailed away he had every reason to feel he had been successful in his new role of instructor of the American people.

But distrust of the British, which had come to the surface during the recent San Mun Bay episode, still lingered, and shortly it received another stimulus. In April, 1899, Great Britain and Russia concluded the so-called Scott-Mouravieff convention. Under its terms the former country agreed not to seek railway concessions north of the Great Wall, in return for a similar Russian promise applicable to the Yangtsze Valley.[37] Here was frank resort by the professed defender of liberal commercial policies to spheres of influence for railways. It was but a short step to spheres for commerce as well, and this would be a deathblow to the Open Door.

The Scott-Mouravieff convention doubtless absorbed the attention of the American-China Development Company. The com-

32. Beresford, *Break-Up of China,* tells about his trip. W. W. Rockhill referred to "the great weight which Beresford's book seems to have with the American people . . ." (Hay papers [MSS in The Library of Congress], Rockhill to Hay, August 28, 1899).

33. New York Chamber of Commerce, *Annual Report* (1898–99), pp. 94, 102–113.

34. Minute-Book of the American Asiatic Association (1898–1919), p. 18.

35. *Literary Digest, 18* (1899), 243; *Public Opinion, 26* (1899), 264.

36. *Journal of Commerce and Commercial Bulletin,* February 25, 1899; see also *Literary Digest, 28* (1899), 243.

37. Rockhill, *Treaties and Conventions,* pp. 183–184.

pany's reaction is unknown, but one may be confident that although welcoming Russia's exclusion from central China it bitterly opposed such a clear-cut move in the direction of spheres of influence. The general reaction in the United States was of course hostile, all the more so since the area reserved for Russia coincided with the principal market for American cotton goods. At least one doughty champion of American rights in China could no longer find reason to look to Britain for assistance. In a speech before the New York Chamber of Commerce John Barrett said flatly: "The move that England has recently made . . . has placed her irrevocably in the category of nations that recognize 'spheres of influence,' . . . which are synonyms of 'areas of actual sovereignty.' " Only the United States, he declared, still stood for commercial equality in China.[38]

A black picture confronted the business interests in the summer of 1899. Many signs pointed to a speedy disintegration of the Chinese Empire. But appearances were deceptive. Thanks in considerable measure to the propaganda of the American Asiatic Association President McKinley and his advisers had come to believe that large and politically influential sections of the American people attached some of their fondest hopes to the Chinese market. The government stood ready to step forth in defense of the Open Door.

38. New York Chamber of Commerce, *Annual Report* (1899–1900), pp. 15–28. The speech was delivered June 1, 1899.

VIII

THE SEPTEMBER NOTES

THE administration of President McKinley in the autumn of 1899 appraised the Chinese market much more highly than it had when John Sherman was secretary of state less than two years before. In the meantime it had become convinced of the considerable value of that market to the United States, a conviction attributable, according to the well-known contemporary writer, Charles A. Conant, mainly to the efforts of the *Journal of Commerce* and the American Asiatic Association.[1] Far from making light of threats to the independence of the Chinese Empire the administration now, as it observed with concern the developing San Mun Bay affair, decided that the time had come to intervene in the Far East in support of the Open Door.

The Russian government may have hastened the decision. By official ukase the tsar on August 11, 1899, proclaimed Talienwan, a city within Russia's sphere in Manchuria, a free port. The ukase had special significance to the United States in that Talienwan was the main port of entry for American cotton goods; it seemed the more significant in view of an article which had just been published in the *North American Review*. Since this article was written by an intimate and influential friend of the tsar's, Prince Esper Oukhtomsky, many Americans were sure that it was officially inspired. Greatly to their surprise it made a strong plea for Russo-American cooperation to maintain the "independence and integrity of China."[2]

At least one acute observer was quick to recognize the meaning the ukase could have for American diplomacy. Alfred Hippisley,[3] a British subject normally resident in China but at the moment

1. *Journal of Commerce and Commercial Bulletin,* April 7, 1899.
2. Vladimir Holmstrem, "Ex Oriente Lux! A Plea for a Russo-American Understanding," *North American Review, 169* (1899), 6–32. Prince Oukhtomsky made his appeal in an introduction to Holmstrem's article.
3. For Hippisley's connection with the formulation of the Open Door Policy see A. W. Griswold, *The Far Eastern Policy of the United States* (New York, Harcourt, Brace & Co., 1938), chap. ii.

visiting the United States, wrote to his American friend W. W. Rockhill, Secretary Hay's adviser on Chinese affairs, that the ukase gave a "natural opportunity" for American intervention in the complicated situation in China.[4] Whether with the ukase in mind or not, Hay did in fact seize the "natural opportunity." On August 24 he asked Rockhill to draft a despatch designed to extract from the great powers a promise to respect "commercial freedom of action" in China.[5]

Although an acknowledged expert on the Far East, Rockhill had not been there for some years. He was in consequence delighted to have the up-to-date information of Hippisley and since early in the summer of 1899 had been exchanging opinions with him on American foreign policy. The two men agreed wholeheartedly on the urgency of a pronouncement by the United States in favor of maintaining the Open Door. Rockhill was also in touch with the American Asiatic Association, of which he became a member in October, 1899.[6] At various times before and after that date he corresponded and had interviews with John Foord, Clarence Cary, Everett Frazar, and other members of the association on matters relating to China.[7] It is reasonable to believe that these contacts, like those with Hippisley, influenced Rockhill's thinking; but there is no evidence that the association made any direct contribution to the memorandum which Rockhill wrote in response to Hay's request. The memorandum was finished on August 28, 1899. It contained some of Hippisley's ideas and even some phrases from an earlier communication from him to Rockhill, and it reflected faithfully the propaganda of the American Asiatic Association. With a few changes part of the memorandum furnished the text of the famous Open Door notes.

At least as early as the end of August, 1899, Secretary Hay was willing to run the political and diplomatic risks attendant upon intervention in China. Was President McKinley similarly

4. Rockhill papers, Hippisley to Rockhill, August 21, 1899; and Rockhill to Hippisley, August 18, 1899.

5. This paragraph is based on Griswold, *Far Eastern Policy,* chap. ii.

6. *The American Asiatic Association, 1900,* pp. 27–32.

7. For evidence that Rockhill was in contact with the association just before he commenced to draft the memorandum on which the September notes were based, see Rockhill papers, Rockhill to Foord, August 18, 1899: "I have somehow mislaid the copy of the program and scope of the Association. Could you send me two or three copies of it, as I am greatly desirous of of [*sic*] showing it to some persons who are deeply interested in the Far Eastern questions." Was not one of these persons perhaps Hippisley?

prepared? If not, another development may have made up his mind for him. Four days after the tsar's ukase Jacob Gould Schurman, head of a commission appointed by the president to make a report on the Philippines,[8] landed at San Francisco. Somewhat surprisingly he told the press: "It seems to me that the great question is not . . . the Philippines, but China. . . . the future of China was the one overwhelming question. China . . . should maintain its independent position, but its doors should be kept open. It means much to England and Japan and not less to America."[9] According to Rockhill Schurman's opinions on China would have "very great influence on the Administration."[10] How great, in fact, was his influence? Were the commissioner's published statements and the advices he expressed privately to President McKinley, with whom he had conversations on September 2 and 4,[11] instrumental in persuading the president to approve the points set forth in Rockhill's memorandum? There seems no way of knowing. But whatever the immediate cause, McKinley's decision—of momentous consequence to the United States—was to approve the policy recommended by his secretary of state.

Accordingly the United States on September 6, 1899, addressed notes [12] to Great Britain, Germany, Russia, France, Italy, and Japan. It asked them to agree

that each, within its respective sphere of whatever influence—

First. Will in no way interfere with any treaty port or any vested interest within any so-called "sphere of interest" or leased territory it may have in China.

Second. That the Chinese treaty tariff of the time being shall apply to all merchandise landed or shipped to all such ports as are within said "sphere of interest" (unless they be "free ports"), no matter to what nationality it may belong, and that duties so leviable shall be collected by the Chinese Government.

Third. That it will levy no higher harbor dues on vessels of another nationality frequenting any port in such "sphere" than shall be levied

8. Charles Denby, the former minister to China, was another member of the commission.

9. *New York Times,* August 16, 1899.

10. Rockhill papers, Rockhill to Hippisley, August 18, 1899; and Rockhill to Adee, August 19, 1899.

11. McKinley papers (MS in the Library of Congress), Schurman to McKinley, August 23, 1899; Cortelyou to Schurman, September 4, 1899.

12. Although the United States did not despatch the notes to France, Italy, and Japan until after September, the term "September notes" will be used for convenience to cover the notes to all six countries.

on vessels of its own nationality, and no higher railroad charges over lines built, controlled, or operated within its "sphere" on merchandise belonging to citizens or subjects of other nationalities transported through such "sphere" than shall be levied on similar merchandise belonging to its own nationals transported over equal distances.[13]

The six countries responded with varying degrees of compliance and pleasure. By what people considered a clever diplomatic stroke, Secretary Hay in acknowledging the replies blandly pretended —what was far from the truth—that all had accepted without reservation the three points contained in the notes.

Here, at last, was a major effort to safeguard equal trading opportunity with China. Most American publications—the business publications with near unanimity—endorsed the government's action.[14] Although the notes explicitly recognized spheres of influence and although they made no reference to the preservation of the independence and integrity of the Chinese Empire, they went far toward meeting the desires of businessmen. Cotton interests, for the moment at least, need not fear tariff discrimination; the American-China Development Company could feel assured that commercial equality would indirectly facilitate investment; and people who had been dreaming of the potential market could now anticipate uninterrupted dreams for many years to come.

The special business interests had further reason for satisfaction in that they believed themselves partly responsible for the decision to send the notes. "We have been in close touch," said the president of the American Asiatic Association, Everett Frazar, when he learned of the American démarche, "both by correspondence with and personal calls upon our Secretary of State . . . in the matter of maintaining the 'open door' in China. . . . We are pleased to note that entire success is likely. . . . It will strengthen

13. *Foreign Relations* (1899), pp. 129–130, Hay to White, September 6, 1899. The quotation is from the note to Great Britain; the notes to the other countries were almost identical.

14. For the reaction of the press see *Harper's Weekly, 43* (1899), 1154; *Literary Digest, 19* (1899), 607; *20* (1900), 35, 415; *Public Opinion, 27* (1899), 643–644; *28* (1900), 10, 37–38. For business sentiment there are no similar compilations; it is necessary to examine the various business periodicals and newspapers. See also *Proceedings of the Thirtieth Annual Meeting of the National Board of Trade,* p. 290; *Proceedings of the Fifth Annual Convention of Manufacturers of the United States of America,* pp. 23–24, 113–114; Department of State, Miscellaneous Letters, April, 1900, Part 1, Lyman to Hay; April 7, 1900; *ibid.,* May, 1900, Part 1, Search to Hay, May 3, 1900.

and stimulate our trade with that great Empire." [15] John Hay in all probability had needed little persuasion. The secretary, as has appeared, had for some time favored commercial equality in China. As for President McKinley, who has been curiously neglected in most accounts of the Open Door Policy, one fact above all is noteworthy: the president was politically dependent on businessmen and a presidential election was due the next year. McKinley had won the bitterly fought election of 1896 as the champion of business, which almost solidly had supported him against the "dangerous" William Jennings Bryan. Hoping for re-election in 1900, he knew that he would have to rely again on this same backing. Certainly McKinley could not afford to alienate such prominent business leaders as those comprising the American Asiatic Association and the American-China Development Company. These men did not allow him to forget his dependence. "With President McKinley and his Cabinet associates, with frequent personal calls and correspondence, we keep in good accord, and . . . our suggestions and resolutions . . . have ever been received with warm appreciation," Everett Frazar declared.[16] There can be little doubt that the repeated and urgent appeals of influential businessmen for support of the Open Door had their effect upon the politically minded president.

Through its branch in Shanghai, too, the Asiatic Association believed that it had made itself felt. The notes demonstrate, declared the president of the American Association of China at a banquet in Shanghai attended by Minister Conger, "that our opinions do meet with consideration, and that we can do good work in furthering the interests of our commercial . . . bodies." [17]

In addition to influencing governmental officials business propaganda had helped to prepare the general public for the September notes. Vigorous intervention in the Far East would probably have been politically impossible well into 1899, but by the autumn of 1899 public opinion had changed noticeably. "There has never," the *Journal of Commerce* asserted in November, "been a more remarkable advance of public sentiment in this country than that which has taken place during the last two years in regard to the responsibilities to be faced by our Government in the Far East." [18]

15. *Asia; Journal of the American Asiatic Association, 1* (1900), 73.
16. *Ibid., 1* (1899), 34.
17. *Ibid., 1* (1900), 87. The dinner was held on November 13, 1899.
18. *Journal of Commerce and Commercial Bulletin,* November 11, 1899.

The main credit for the "remarkable advance" was due, the *Journal* considered, to its own efforts and to those of John Barrett and of the American Asiatic Association.[19] James S. Fearon, partner in Fearon, Daniel and Company and for many years chairman of the Shanghai Municipal Council, expressed an almost identical opinion.[20]

Such assertions must not be accepted uncritically. Business propaganda, however important, was not the only factor conditioning McKinley's administration in favor of the Open Door Policy.[21] Nonetheless a careful appraisal of the evidence leads to an inescapable conclusion: the pressure which the special business interests brought to bear upon the government, principally through the American Asiatic Association, had major importance in bringing about the decision to send the notes of September 6, 1899.

19. *Ibid.,* October 19, 1899; January 27, 1900.

20. *Ibid.,* October 27, 1899. Fearon attributed the credit to the *Journal of Commerce* and to the American Asiatic Association.

21. For an account of political and diplomatic influences see Griswold, *Far Eastern Policy,* chap. ii.

IX

FURTHER PRESSURE

THE September notes, however welcome, did not entirely satisfy the business interests. In the opinion of many businessmen Hay had made the immeasurable mistake of failing to require a guarantee of Chinese political and territorial integrity. It was obvious to them that complete partition of the Chinese Empire would be perfectly in accord with the terms of the notes, provided only that over the same area commercial equality for all continued to prevail. It is not surprising, therefore, that between the time of the September notes and the circular of July 3, 1900, businessmen should have clamored for a broadening and strengthening of Far Eastern policy.

Expressions of gratitude for the September notes were frequently coupled with regrets over their neglect of provisions relative to China's independence and integrity. A convention of cotton spinners resolved in November, 1899, in favor of "the preservation of the integrity of the Chinese empire"; [1] and the National Board of Trade at its annual convention in early 1900 expressed "firm conviction that the United States should use all the influence it can . . . to prevent . . . a cutting-up . . . of the Chinese Empire." [2] The American Asiatic Association regarded the notes as "merely the first step towards the permanent establishment of the open door"; there were still many goals, it declared, to be sought, "chief among them being the preservation of the integrity of the Chinese Empire itself." Far from disbanding, it thought it "certain that there is more important work before the association even than any it has yet undertaken." [3]

Numerous other statements, while not explicitly referring to Chinese integrity, left no doubts as to the continuing desire for firmness in the Far East. The cotton interests, both northern and

1. *Journal of Commerce and Commercial Bulletin,* November 3, 1899; *Bradstreet's, 28* (1899), 689.
2. *Proceedings of the Thirteenth Annual Meeting of the National Board of Trade,* p. 290.
3. *The American Asiatic Association, 1900,* p. 20.

southern, persistently advocated resolute action. A convention of the New England Cotton Manufacturers' Association meeting in October, 1899, applauded enthusiastically a plea for cooperation with Great Britain and Japan to preserve the Open Door.[4] In the same month the cotton spinners of South Carolina enjoined upon their congressmen the protection of trade with China; this trade, they pointed out, absorbed nearly the entire output of South Carolina's cotton mills.[5] Senators and representatives hastened to give assurances; "utmost endeavors," money, and men, one senator promised, would be devoted to making China safe for his constituents.[6] The Southern Cotton Spinners' Association, assembled in Charlotte, North Carolina, in November, 1899, noted the remarkable increase during the preceding decade in exports of "surplus" cotton goods to the Chinese Empire and resolved: "That we urge upon the President of the United States and on Senators and Representatives in Congress the . . . preservation of . . . all our treaty rights with that empire, and the maintenance of an 'open door' policy in China." Echoing John Barrett, who four days previously had delivered an address in Charlotte,[7] they further urged the immediate construction of an Isthmian canal and of a Pacific cable as well as the establishment of permanent control over the Philippines. These steps, they argued, were required to consolidate commercial relations with China.[8]

Like the cotton-goods industry the American-China Development Company continued to press for strong measures. Since the day in February, 1899, when it had reached agreement with the British and Chinese Corporation [9] the American company had been having its usual troubles. About two months before the September-notes were sent its chief engineer, W. B. Parsons (a member of the American Asiatic Association), called on Secretary Hay. China, Parsons said, was making difficulties about the company's request for certain revisions of the contract; [10] and Clarence Cary, whom the company had felt obliged to send to

4. *Transactions of the New England Cotton Manufacturers' Association*, Nos. 67, 69. These statements were made before public knowledge of the September notes. Official notice of the notes came in January, 1900, but in November, 1899, there was a widely credited report of their despatch.

5. *Senate Document*, No. 230, 56th Congress, First Session, pp. 6–7.

6. *Journal of Commerce and Commercial Bulletin*, October 16, 17, 1899.

7. *Ibid.*, October 30, 1899.

8. *Ibid.*, November 3, 1899; *Bradstreet's, 28* (1899), 689.

9. See p. 40.

10. *Journal of Commerce and Commercial Bulletin*, July 15, 1899.

China a second time, had just telegraphed that failure was imminent unless the American government intervened. Hay sympathized with Parsons' appeal for official backing.[11] He at once wired to Minister Conger: ". . . use your good offices energetically in behalf of American-China Development Company . . ." [12] Conger carried out this instruction faithfully. He accompanied Cary to the Chinese Foreign Office where he vigorously asserted the company's interpretation of the contract; [13] and a little later he went to Hankow to tell the powerful viceroy there that the United States insisted upon respect for the concern's rights.[14] But despite the minister's urgings and despite a second instruction from Hay to "use good offices," [15] the Chinese still refused to meet the company's terms.[16]

It was not only the cotton interests and the American-China Development Company but the business community as a whole which continued to show deep concern over the fate of China. In the autumn of 1899 the Philadelphia Commercial Museum sponsored a so-called International Commercial Congress, a large assembly in Philadelphia of many Americans as well as delegates of 41 foreign governments and 164 foreign chambers of commerce and trade organizations.[17] Backed by the United States government, which had transmitted the invitations, the congress attracted widespread attention. The American Asiatic Association had charge of the session on China. One of its members, Cornelius N. Bliss, the former secretary of the interior, presided. Delegates from the chambers of commerce of Shanghai, Hongkong, and London gave addresses, as did Everett Frazar, John Barrett, and Wu Ting Fang, China's minister at Washington. All the speakers stressed the urgent need for the United States to do everything in its power to strengthen the Open Door.

Frequent appeals were made in the period between the Septem-

11. Department of State, Miscellaneous Letters, July, 1899, Part 2, Whitridge to Hay, July 13, 1899.

12. *Idem,* Instructions, China, *6,* 3, telegram, Hay to Conger, July 14, 1899; *idem,* Despatches, China, *106,* No. 235, Conger to Hay, July 15, 1899.

13. *Idem,* Despatches, China, *107,* No. 288, enclosure, Cary to Conger, November 20, 1899; *ibid.,* Conger to Hay, December 6, 1899.

14. *Ibid.,* No. 302, Conger to Hay, December 31, 1899.

15. *Idem,* Instructions, China, *6,* 72, Hay to Conger, May 7, 1900; *idem,* Miscellaneous Letters, May, 1900, Part 2, Whitridge to Hay, May 12, 1900.

16. See Cary's lament in *idem,* Despatches, China, *107,* No. 278, enclosure, Cary to Whitridge, September 3, 1899.

17. For a full account of the congress see *Official Proceedings of the International Commercial Congress,* published by the Philadelphia Commercial Museum, 1899.

ber notes and the July circular for reform of the consular service, often on the ground that thereby trade with China would be promoted.[18] Early in 1900 representatives of commercial bodies of New York, Cleveland, and Chicago as well as of several national business organizations testified before congressional committees on various proposals for reform. The American Association of China wrote to Hay in support of a measure prepared by the New York and Cleveland chambers of commerce and by the National Business League of Chicago in consultation with the State Department: "We have learned with great satisfaction," the asssociation stated, "of the triumph of our diplomacy in securing guarantees from the other Treaty Powers of the 'Open-Door' policy in this country [China]. A re-organized Consular Service . . . would . . . contribute in large degree towards enabling us to avail [sic] of the free entrance for our trade to the best advantage." [19] Although no measure passed at the time, the subject of reform continued to occupy the attention of business organizations through 1900. Indirectly the agitation helped to focus attention on China.

Two rather trifling incidents served the same purpose; both related to Shanghai. The Whang Poo River on which that city is situated having become filled with silt, the Shanghai Chamber of Commerce asked W. W. Rockhill as well as the New York Chamber of Commerce to use their influence toward getting the channel dug out. Rockhill, approving, passed the request to Hay; [20] and the New York Chamber urged the secretary to take up the matter with the Chinese: the "rapid expansion" of American commerce with China, it declared, made action a "necessity." [21] In response Hay instructed Conger to "do what you properly can to further the wishes of the petitioners." [22] The second incident was the establishment at Shanghai by the National Association of Manufacturers of an American warehouse, intended to supersede a rather unsuccessful one set up some years before by the Manufacturers' Association of Philadelphia. Within a short time about a hundred

18. See p. 3.

19. Department of State, Miscellaneous Letters, April, 1900, Part 1, Lyman to Hay, April 7, 1900.

20. *Ibid.,* December, 1899, Part 1, Rockhill to Hay, December 1, 1899.

21. New York Chamber of Commerce, *Annual Report* (1898–1900), pp. 41, 73–74, the Chamber to Hay, December 9, 1899.

22. Department of State, Instructions, China, *6,* No. 220, Hay to Conger, December 18, 1899.

American business firms had applied for exhibition space in the new warehouse.[23]

Of greater significance was a recurrence of the agitation for a commercial commission to study opportunities for business with China. In his annual message for 1899 President McKinley reminded Congress of former Secretary Day's proposal to appoint such a commission and of his own request in December, 1898.[24] "I now renew this recommendation," he said, "as the importance of the subject has steadily grown since it was first submitted to you, and no time should be lost in studying for ourselves the resources of this great field for American trade and enterprise." [25] Within a month five bills were under the scrutiny of various congressional committees.[26]

Businessmen for well over a year and a half had been advocating a commercial commission. They favored, apparently with near unanimity, a bill sponsored by Senator Gallinger and Representative Hepburn; and many of them put pressure on the government to secure its adoption.[27] The New York Board of Trade and Transportation [28] and the New York Chamber of Commerce [29] wrote to every member of Congress urging passage of the bill; and the Boston Chamber of Commerce despatched several communications to the congressmen from Massachusetts.[30] The boards of trade of Cleveland, Chicago, Boston, St. Louis, and Philadelphia went further: they sent witnesses to testify before the Foreign Affairs Committee of the House.[31] John Barrett was another earnest witness.[32] The National Board of Trade,[33] the Trans-Mississippi

23. For the early history of the warehouse see *Proceedings of the Fifth Annual Convention of the National Association of Manufacturers of the United States of America*, pp. 25–26; *Journal of Commerce and Commercial Bulletin*, August 29, 1899; *House Report*, No. 484, 56th Congress, First Session, p. 5; *Senate Report*, No. 450, 56th Congress, First Session, p. 7; Boston Chamber of Commerce, *Annual Report* (1900), pp. 22, 130.

24. See p. 38.

25. *Foreign Relations* (1899), p. xviii.

26. One of the bills was drafted by W. W. Rockhill and sponsored by Senator Henry Cabot Lodge. See Rockhill papers, Emory to Rockhill, December 16, 1899; "Memorandum," December 20, 1899; Rockhill to Lodge, December 25, 1899.

27. *Congressional Record, 33*, 4876.

28. *Senate Report*, No. 450, 56th Congress, First Session, p. 7.

29. *Ibid.;* see also New York Chamber of Commerce, *Annual Report* (1899–1900), p. 84.

30. Boston Chamber of Commerce, *Annual Report* (1900), pp. 22, 130.

31. *Congressional Record, 33*, 4881.

32. *Journal of Commerce and Commercial Bulletin*, January 20, 1900.

33. *Congressional Record, 33*, 4881.

Commercial Congress,[34] and the Southern Cotton Spinners' Association [35] added their exhortations; while the United States Export Association informed Congress that its members, representing ninety-eight principal lines of industry in thirty-four states, were "without exception . . . strongly in favor" of the Gallinger-Hepburn bill.[36]

Another zealous supporter was the National Association of Manufacturers. By establishing its warehouse in Shanghai this influential business organization, which included in its membership over eleven hundred of the largest industries in the country, had already given proof of keen desire to foster commercial relations with China. The association resolved in favor of the Gallinger-Hepburn bill in January [37] and again at its annual convention in April.[38] Moreover its president, Theodore C. Search, insisted in letters to Senator Gallinger and Representative Hepburn that China could "furnish a market for millions upon millions of dollars' worth of American products." He followed up this appeal in frequent conferences with the bill's sponsors.[39]

The American Asiatic Association of course concerned itself in this matter so intimately connected with trade with China. Eager to have its own members represented on the proposed commission,[40] the association lost no time in enlisting the support of other business organizations [41] and in exerting pressure on Washington. Early in February John Foord, J. S. Fearon, and Clarence Cary, just back from his second trip to the Far East, conferred at the Cosmos Club in Washington with W. W. Rockhill, who, rumor said, was destined to head the commission.[42] There these men, all so influential in matters of Far Eastern policy, decided upon appropriate measures for securing the kind of body they wanted. The next month in New York Foord again discussed the matter with Rockhill.[43] The association was also working through other

34. *Ibid.;* see also *Official Proceedings of the Eighth Convention of the Trans-Mississippi Commercial Congress,* pp. 22, 217.
35. *Journal of Commerce and Commercial Bulletin,* May 12, 1900.
36. *House Report,* No. 484, 56th Congress, First Session, pp. 4–5.
37. *Ibid.*
38. *Proceedings of the Fifth Annual Convention of the National Association of Manufacturers of the United States of America,* p. 151.
39. *Senate Report,* No. 450, 56th Congress, First Session, pp. 4, 8.
40. Minute-Book of the American Asiatic Association (1898–1919), pp. 42–43.
41. *Ibid.,* pp. 34–35, 37, 41.
42. *Ibid.,* p. 33; Rockhill papers, Foord to Rockhill, February 6, 1900, and Rockhill to Foord, February 7, 1900.
43. *Ibid.,* Rockhill to Foord, March 5, 1900. A quotation from this letter shows

officials in Washington. Its president, Everett Frazar, kept in close touch with various members of Congress, notably Senators Frye, McLaurin,[44] Hanna, and Lodge, and also with the assistant secretary of state, Secretary Hay, and President McKinley.[45] Frazar seems to have had sympathetic hearings from all these men.

As regards the proposed commercial commission, the influence of business is obvious. Businessmen favored the Gallinger-Hepburn bill, and that was the one the congressional committees reported favorably. Both Senator Gallinger [46] and Representative Hepburn [47] declared that they had introduced their measure in response to business requests. The bill passed the Senate on March 24, 1900. Whether it would have passed the House, and if it had, whether the commission would have been such as the American Asiatic Association favored, cannot be known. Before the final vote alarming news came from China.

The antiforeign outbreaks which had caused American gunboats to hasten to China in 1898 and German troops to invade Shantung province in 1899 had by 1900 become extremely serious. So violent was the agitation against western "barbarians" that in the spring the United States and certain European countries felt compelled to order troops to Peking. In such circumstances prospects for commerce faded. Despite the Open Door notes of 1899 the potential market confronted a new danger, in some ways a greater one than ever before. Inevitably attention shifted from the projected commission; it would be devoid of meaning until law and order returned to the stricken Chinese Empire.

But even though in the emergency Congress set aside the Gallinger-Hepburn bill, the campaign for a commission had served a real purpose. By evoking a veritable storm of support it had demonstrated beyond all doubt that businessmen continued to have high regard for the vast market across the Pacific and that they

---

the close connection between the two men: "I read with great interest the editorial in your paper [the *Journal of Commerce*] on the subject of the commercial commission and fully concur with your views."

44. Senator McLaurin, representing South Carolina which was particularly interested in the cotton trade with China, could always be relied on to support business wishes on matters relating to the Far East (*Asia; Journal of the American Asiatic Association, 2* [1901], 114).

45. *Journal of Commerce and Commercial Bulletin,* March 17, 1900.

46. *Senate Report,* No. 450, 56th Congress, First Session, p. 5.

47. *House Report,* No. 484, 56th Congress, First Session, p. 1. See also *Congressional Record, 33,* 4881, where it is recorded "that the bill has been introduced . . . under pressure from the business and manufacturing interests of this country."

were ready for a stronger policy than the one delineated in the September notes. The campaign had confirmed the many lesser but still potent indications of business opinion—such as the activities of the National Association of Manufacturers, the promptings of the cotton-goods industry, the recurrent appeals of the American-China Development Company, and the vigilance of the American Asiatic Association. With so much evidence the government could proceed, when the opportunity arose in the summer of 1900, to yet further intervention in the Far East. It could do so with the assurance of increasing its popularity among the business interests on which its political fortunes depended. Such assurance was of paramount importance to all politicians in the presidential election year of 1900.

X

THE JULY CIRCULAR

DURING the last few years of the nineteenth century anti-foreign sentiment in China was growing rapidly. Two secret societies cooperated effectively to stir up animosity against the encroaching "barbarian." Of the two the Righteous and Harmonious Band, commonly but incorrectly known to non-Chinese as the Boxers,[1] was by far the more dangerous. Enjoying the secret sympathy and support of numerous officials of the Chinese government including the empress dowager herself, the society by the beginning of 1900 had built itself to formidable strength.[2]

Throughout the winter of 1900 the Boxers busied themselves with scattered assaults on foreigners and native Christians. Rumors were rife of an imminent general uprising.[3] In the spring the attacks became more frequent. To protect their nationals several of the great powers in May, 1900, sent troops to the legation area in Peking. The Boxers now threw off all restraint. They laid siege to the legations, severed their communications with the sea, and slaughtered several hundred foreigners in various parts of the empire. In June the Chinese government declared war on much of the western world.

These shocking events terrified many American businessmen. Surveying the national reaction the *Literary Digest* found that despite the anxiety over the besieged legations "the *commercial* aspect" of the turmoil in China was very much in people's minds.[4] Traders no longer had their market; prospective investors such as the American-China Development Company were brought to

1. G. N. Steiger, *China and the Occident, the Origin and Development of the Boxer Movement* (New Haven, 1927), p. 134, shows that the word "Boxer" resulted from an inaccurate translation of the Chinese. The other secret society was the Great Sword Society.

2. When no source is cited the material dealing with the Boxers is based on Steiger, *China and the Occident*.

3. See *Foreign Relations* (1900), pp. 139–141, for a despatch from Conger sounding the alarm.

4. *Literary Digest, 20* (1900), 744; author's italics.

a halt; those looking to the potential market stood revealed as apparent victims of gross self-deception. Since the disorders centered in north China and Manchuria it was above all the cotton-goods industry which was endangered. Orders fell off; some mills began to install machinery for production of finer goods than those exported to China; fewer new mills were projected.[5] The *Journal of Commerce*, that zealous watchdog over the cotton trade, published one frantic editorial after another insisting, it is scarcely necessary to say, on action by the United States. A government publication stated that it was "a matter of the first importance for those American cotton manufacturers in the South who depend almost exclusively on the Chinese demand that normal relations with that Empire should be resumed";[6] and the *Chicago Inter Ocean*, referring to the greatly decreased exports of cotton manufactures in May, 1900, explained: "That is why . . . tens of thousands of American working men are interested in having our Government do its share to bring back East Asia from utter anarchy."[7]

Faced with this emergency which threatened all its accomplishments and hopes the American Asiatic Association braced itself for a supreme effort. Already, as early as March 16, its president Everett Frazar had consulted with President McKinley, in part about the commercial commission (at that date still under consideration by Congress), but also, it appears, about the menacing situation in the Far East.[8] The day before, the association's branch in Shanghai had telegraphed to Secretary Hay that only immediate concerted action by the powers could prevent China from lapsing into such conditions as would nullify the recent Open Door notes.[9] In all probability Frazar discussed this grim warning with the president.

Early in June a disturbing cable from its Shanghai office reached the Asiatic Association: "American lives and interests in North China are seriously imperiled. Urge Government to act promptly and vigorously with adequate force."[10] The long simmering out-

---

5. *Ibid., 21* (1900), 62, quotes the *Chicago Inter Ocean* to the effect that the uprising entirely stopped the Pepperell cotton mills' exports to China.

6. *Commercial Relations* (1900), I, 43.

7. *Literary Digest, 21* (1900), 62.

8. *Journal of Commerce and Commercial Bulletin,* March 17, 20, 1900.

9. Department of State, Miscellaneous Letters, March, 1900, Part 2, to Hay, March 15, 1900.

10. *Ibid.,* June, 1900, Part 1, Cary, Frazar, and Foord to Hay, June 8, 1900.

break had commenced. On receipt of the bad news the association immediately called an emergency meeting of the executive committee. The committee decided upon three steps. First, over the signatures of Clarence Cary, Everett Frazar, and John Foord it reported to the secretary of state the contents of the message from Shanghai.[11] Second, it drew up a memorial demanding of the government "prompt and vigorous application of adequate force" in China, if necessary "in concert with other Powers."[12] It mailed copies to various businessmen with the earnest request that they sign them and return them for transmission to the State Department. Third, the committee sent its indefatigable secretary, John Foord, to Washington for conferences with Hay.[13] Presumably Foord impressed upon the secretary of state the gravity of the Chinese situation and the pressing need of stern measures.

Hardly was this mission accomplished when another cable arrived from the American Association of China: "Grave danger threatens Americans at Yangtzse [sic] Valley. Urgently advise immediate gunboat protection."[14] Foord again hurried to the capital for discussions with Hay. Almost as he went there came a fourth cable, a startling one raising the ominous question of whether Russia had a hand in the disorders: "The situation is serious. The Chinese Government is believed to be supported by Russia in concert with the Boxers. It is absolutely essential that America should continue to act in concert with other powers in opposition to Russia. It is absolutely essential to send as soon as possible a larger force. Bring all the pressure you can to bear on our Government."[15] If Russia should in truth be involved, the policy set forth in the September notes might collapse altogether. The Asiatic Association immediately informed Secretary Hay of its somber news.[16] It also reassured the Shanghai office as to its harmonious collaboration with the authorities in Washington.[17]

By June 18 the Asiatic Association had got back most of the copies of its memorial duly signed, and considering immediate

11. *Ibid.*

12. *Ibid.,* Part 2, Foord to McKinley, June 18, 1900; Minute-Book of the American Asiatic Association (1898–1919), pp. 46–47, 49; *Journal of Commerce and Commercial Bulletin,* June 15, 1900.

13. Minute-Book of the American Asiatic Association (1898–1919), p. 46.

14. *Journal of Commerce and Commercial Bulletin,* June 15, 1900.

15. Department of State, Miscellaneous Letters, June, 1900, Part 2, Foord to Hay, June 15, 1900.

16. *Journal of Commerce and Commercial Bulletin,* June 16, 1900.

17. Minute-Book of the American Asiatic Association (1898–1919), p. 49.

action imperative it despatched the lot to President McKinley. Signers included such cotton exporters as Frazar and Company, Fearon, Daniel and Company, and Deering, Milliken and Company; such members of the American-China Development Company as Clarence Cary and W. B. Parsons; and such other business concerns and businessmen as the Equitable Life Assurance Society, the Guaranty Trust Company, the United States Export Association, the Baldwin Locomotive Works, the Rogers Locomotive Company, W. P. Wilson (director of the Philadelphia Commercial Museum), and John Barrett.[18] After receiving this large batch of memorials demanding "prompt and vigorous application of adequate force," the administration could be more confident than ever of enthusiastic business support of a bold policy.

But despite the assurance the government was not yet ready to intervene. Believing further pressure necessary the American Asiatic Association immediately began to prepare a second memorial.[19] Moreover, for a third time John Foord went to Washington where he conferred with W. W. Rockhill and David J. Hill, assistant secretary of state, as well as with his recent and sympathetic listener, John Hay.[20] With reports from the Far East becoming increasingly alarming, the association on June 27 once again spurred on the State Department: it was "impossible," it wrote, "to exaggerate the gravity of the situation." [21] By that time the Boxers had assassinated the German minister; suspicions of Russia filled the American press; and all the fears which had been lulled by the September notes were springing back to life.[22]

Another organization which felt deep anxiety was the American-China Development Company. Unless favorable conditions re-

18. For the complete list of signers see Department of State, Miscellaneous Letters, June, 1900, Part 2, Foord to McKinley, June 18, 1900; *ibid.*, Part 3, Foord to Cortelyou, June 22, 1900. The Asiatic Association asked W. W. Rockhill to sign the memorial. Although the memorial had his "hearty approval," he thought it improper for him as a government official to do so (Rockhill papers, Rockhill to Foord, June 11, 1900).

19. Department of State, Miscellaneous Letters, July, 1900, Part 1, Foord to Hay, July 3, 1900; *ibid.*, Part 2, Lyman to McKinley, July 20, 1900; Minute-Book of the American Asiatic Association (1898–1919), p. 51.

20. *Journal of Commerce and Commercial Bulletin,* June 29, 1900.

21. Department of State, Miscellaneous Letters, June, 1900, Part 3, Foord to Hay, June 27, 1900. For reference to still other communications which the American Asiatic Association and its branch in Shanghai sent to Washington at the time, see Minute-Book of the American Asiatic Association (1898–1919), p. 51.

22. *Literary Digest, 20* (1900), 777.

emerged in China the prospects of this concern no less than those of the cotton-goods industry were dismal indeed. As has appeared, Clarence Cary in June, 1900, appealed for action against the Boxers. Although he took this step in his capacity as a member of the executive committee of the American Asiatic Association, he could hardly have been without thought of advantage to the Development Company's railway concession, an interest always dear to him. Hard upon Cary's appeal came yet another plea, this one from A. W. Bash, at the moment recuperating in America from his frustrating experiences with the Chinese. Heartily endorsing the stand of the American Asiatic Association Bash demanded of Secretary Hay "a strong policy . . . for the protection of life and property, and the safeguard of the large investments planned, and a considerable portion of which has been already made through the organization, *'The American-China Development Company'* . . ." [23]

In July such a "strong policy" was at last forthcoming. The presidential election was then only four months away, but McKinley and his advisers had seen evidence in abundance of widespread desire in business circles for intervention in China. They could be sure of enthusiastic support from this influential section of the electorate. The steps which the government decided upon were energetic and far-reaching. In the first place, it ordered some five thousand soldiers to China; many of them participated in an international expedition that succeeded in cutting its way to Peking and on August 14 relieving the besieged legation area. Second, on July 3 it addressed a circular letter to the great powers. The letter stated in part: "The policy of the Government of the United States is to seek a solution which may bring about permanent safety and peace to China, preserve Chinese territorial and administrative entity, protect all rights guaranteed to friendly powers by treaty and international law, and safeguard for the world the principle of equal and impartial trade with all parts of the Chinese Empire." [24] To the delight of the special business interests the principle of "Chinese territorial and administrative entity" took its place beside the points enunciated in the September notes. The Open Door Policy of the United States in its essential features was now complete.

23. Department of State, Miscellaneous Letters, June, 1900, Part 2, Bash to Hay, June 15, 1900; italics in original.

24. *Foreign Relations* (1901), App., p. 12.

Thus success appeared to have crowned the efforts of the business interests. They had urged support of the integrity of China. The government had responded with the July circular. With the collapse of the Boxer movement the cotton-goods industry, the American-China Development Company, and the other concerns operating in China could resume business with every hope of success. Behind them—in marked contrast to the days of Secretary Sherman—stood the government of the United States, now committed to a vigorous Open Door Policy.

The reaction of businessmen to the July circular fulfilled expectations. Like the September notes the circular won immediate and enthusiastic approval.[25] Cotton exporters, of course, had particular cause for elation. For a few months they had lost their market in north China. Now it seemed they were about to regain it. Overjoyed, thirty-seven manufacturers of cotton goods expressed to the government "their approval of the action of the United States . . . in the protection of American interests in China, known as the 'open door' policy." [26]

Ten days after the despatch of the circular letter the American-China Development Company at last got the revised contract so long and so arduously pursued. The Chinese minister, still representing his country at Washington in spite of the technical state of war,[27] signed the final papers on July 13, 1900.[28] Although proof is lacking of any causal relationship between this event and the circular of July 3, a remark by Alfred Hippisley suggests the existence of such a connection. Shortly after the sending of the September notes the Englishman wrote to his friend, W. W. Rockhill, that China could hardly decline to conclude the contract much longer "in view of what American diplomacy is doing for her." [29] If such a conjecture appeared reasonable to a highly qualified observer in 1899, it had far more force in mid-July, 1900, when the United States had moved a second time to the defense of China. It is by no means impossible that the Chinese minister

25. In addition to the various business periodicals see Department of State, Miscellaneous Letters, November, 1900, Part 2, Aubrey to Hay, November 16, 1900; *Transactions of the New England Cotton Manufacturers' Association,* October 18, 1900; Minute-Book of the American Asiatic Association (1898–1919), p. 63.

26. *Senate Document,* No. 79, 56th Congress, Second Session, p. 1. The letter as published is not dated; the Senate ordered that it be printed on January 9, 1901.

27. Technically the powers were at war with China until September, 1901 (Steiger, *China and the Occident,* chap. xii).

28. Rockhill, *Treaties and Conventions,* pp. 259–277.

29. Rockhill papers, Hippisley to Rockhill, November 4, 1899.

and perhaps certain other high Chinese officials, grateful for American aid and realizing their country's pressing need of influential friends if it were to escape severe chastisement, decided to award the contract to the American-China Development Company. They may have reasoned that this would give a strong incentive both to the Development Company and to its collaborator, the British and Chinese Association, to caution their governments against partition or any other treatment of China likely to render the new contract inoperative.

The American Asiatic Association, highly gratified by the government's complete acceptance of its recommendations (the association, as will be recalled, had advised "adequate force . . . in concert with other Powers," and the maintenance of China's integrity), was quick to inform Secretary Hay of its "profound satisfaction . . . particularly at the definite statement that the United States Government is opposed to the partition of China." [30] The association claimed much of the credit for the firm American stand in the Far East. "I do not hesitate to predict," its vice-president, S. D. Brewster, triumphantly declared in a speech in New York, "that the work of this Association will take its place in history as part of one of the most memorable chapters in the annals of the American people." Brewster went on to summarize the association's accomplishments in recent years:

In the latter part of 1897 some of the great governments of Europe began to acquire . . . "spheres of influence" in . . . China. It was the belief in the minds of some of the present members of this Association that such action . . . might have serious results for our commerce. This conviction led to the organization of the American Asiatic Association. . . . I think it only just to our Association to say that through all the great events of the past three years we have been watchful of every opportunity to protect and expand the commercial opportunities of the United States in the markets of the Far East. . . . You have only to compare the state of public sentiment which we found existing in regard to the responsibilities of our country in Eastern Asia with the feeling which exists on that subject today to appreciate what the influence of this Association has been. . . . The President and the Secretary of State and other officers of the Government have been pleased to acknowledge the good results of our labors.[31]

30. Department of State, Miscellaneous Letters, August, 1900, Part 2, Foord to Hay, August 21, 1900.
31. *Asia; Journal of the American Asiatic Association,* 2 (1901), 5. Brewster's speech was delivered on May 16, 1901.

Brewster's statement was not exaggerated. The promptings of special business interests often working through the American Asiatic Association constituted one of the main reasons for the despatch of the September notes and the July circular. Business pressure must, as Brewster said, "take its place in history" as part of the explanation of the Open Door Policy.

APPENDIX

The members of the American Asiatic Association as of November 14, 1900 (other than those listed on p. 43 of the text) were the following:

Abbeville Cotton Mills, Abbeville, S. C.

Abendroth and Root Manufacturing Co., New York

Frederick H. Allen, New York

George Marshall Allen, New York

The American Cotton Co., New York

American Lithographic Co., New York

American Steel and Wire Co., New York

Herbert Appleton, New York

Arnhold, Karberg and Co., New York

Atchison, Topeka and Santa Fé R. R. Co., New York

Austin, Nichols and Co., New York

Joshua L. Bailey and Co., New York

William H. Bailey, New York

The Barber Asphalt Paving Co., New York

Barber and Co., New York

Peter T. Barlow, New York

George Clinton Batcheller, New York

Truston Beale, Washington, D. C.

The Bethlehem Steel Co., South Bethlehem, Pa.

Blackall and Baldwin, New York

Bliss, Fabyan and Co., New York

Boorum and Pease, New York

Braeburn Steel Co., Braeburn, Pa.

W. K. Brice, New York

R. von Briesen, New York

J. G. Brill and Co., Philadelphia

Brooks Locomotive Works, Dunkirk, New York

Brown Bros. and Co., Boston

Burnham, Williams and Co., Philadelphia

Busk and Jevons, New York

W. J. Buttfield, New York

L. Camera, Shanghai

Canadian Pacific R. R. Co., New York

I. Osgood Carleton, New York

Carnegie Steel Co., New York

Carter, Macy and Co., New York

Ernest Carter, New York

Clarence Cary, New York

John C. Cary, Lockhart, S. C.

C. and C. Electric Co., New York

Catlin and Co., New York

Central Trust Co., New York

Champion and Staudinger, New York

China and Japan Trading Co., New York

George C. Cholwell and Co., New York

Chubb and Son, New York

H. B. Claflin Co., New York

E. E. Clapp and Co., New York

Colt's Patented Fire Arms Manufacturing Co., Hartford, Conn.

Cooke Locomotive and Machine Co., Patterson, N. J.

E. D. Cordes and Co., New York

Charles de Cordova, New York

Crescent Steel Co., New York
Dwight P. Cruickshank, New York
T. B. Dallas, Nashville, Pa.
John W. Danielson, Providence, R. I.
Darlington Manufacturing Co., Darlington, S. C.
Deering, Milliken and Co., New York
Delacamp and Co., New York
Diamond State Car Springs Co., Wilmington, Del.
Diamond State Steel Co., Wilmington, Del.
Francis E. Dodge, New York
Driggs-Seaburr Gun and Ammunition Co., New York
Edge Moor Bridge Works, Edge Moor, Del.
Ehrich Bros., New York
Fairbanks Co., New York
Fearon, Daniel and Co., New York
J. H. Flagg, New York
Flint Eddy and American Trading Co., New York
John Foord, New York
Francis Blackwall Forbes, Boston, Mass.
Alfred Fraser, New York
Fraser and Chalmers, Inc., New York
Frazar and Co., New York
Funch, Edye and Co., New York
W. Scott Fitz, Boston, Mass.
Goulds Manufacturing Co., Seneca Falls, New York
Henry S. Grew, Boston, Mass.
H. A. Gross, New York
W. and L. E. Gurley, Troy, New York
Haines and Bishop, New York
George Hamilton, New York
J. Wheeler Hardley, New York
Harlan and Hollingsworth Co., Wilmington, Del.

The Hartley Co., New York
Hayward and Wreaks, New York
J. R. Herod, New York
Hewlett and Lee, New York
George F. Hicks, New York
Samuel Hill, Minneapolis
J. W. Hoffman and Co., Philadelphia
Robert W. Hunt and Co., Chicago
Illinois Steel Co., New York
International Express Co., New York
Irwin, McBridge, Catherwood and Co., New York
Gen. Lloyd L. Jackson, Baltimore
Jackson and Sharp Co., Wilmington, Del.
Jones and Laughlin, New York
H. W. Jones Manufacturing Co., New York
Kearney and Foot Co., New York
John Kissock and Co., New York
Kurtz, Stuboeck and Co., New York
Lackawanna Iron and Steel Co., New York
Ladenburg, Thalmann and Co., New York
George W. Lane and Co., New York
Edwin Langdon, New York
A. T. Leftwich, Baltimore
Lewinson and Just, New York
John A. Livermore, New York
Laurus Loomis, New York
H. W. T. Mali and Co., New York
Newell Martin, New York
McConway and Torley Co., Pittsburgh
William McKinley, Jr., New York
Mills Manufacturing Co., Greenville, S. C.
Minot, Hooper and Co., New York
George B. Moffat, New York
James and John Montgomery and Co., New York
George L. Montgomery, New York

Morewood and Co., New York

Henry G. Morse, Wilmington, Del.

Mosle Bros., New York

Thornton N. Motley Co., New York

Mourilyan, Heimann and Co., New York

Naylor and Co., New York

Neuss, Hesslein and Co., New York

Neptune Meter Co., New York

New England Watch Co., Waterbury, Conn.

New York Air Brake Co., New York

New York Leather Belting Co., New York

De Lancey Nicoll, New York

Niles Tool Co., New York

A. Norden and Co., New York

Northern Pacific R. R. Co., New York

Noyes, Bauscher and Gerrish, New York

O'Donohue and Co., New York

Occidental and Oriental S. S. Co., San Francisco

Oelrichs and Co., New York

The Okonite Co., New York

Otis, McAllister and Co., San Francisco

Pacific Mail S. S. Co., San Francisco

Pacolet Manufacturing Co., Pacolet, S. C.

Pantarote Leather Co., New York

Parker, Wilder and Co., New York

S. L. Parrish, New York

William Barclay Parsons, New York

Passavant and Co., New York

Adolph Pavenstedt, New York

Henry W. Peabody and Co., New York

Pennsylvania R. R. Co., New York

Edward Perry, New York

Phelps, Dodge and Co., New York

Philadelphia Commercial Museum, Philadelphia

Phoenix Bridge Co., New York

Phoenix Consolidated Copper Co., New York

Phoenix Silk Manufacturing Co., Patterson, N. J.

Capt. A. E. Piorkowski, New York

J. S. Plummer and Co., New York

Robert P. Porter, New York

Alfred H. Post, New York

E. C. Potter, Chicago

Putnam, Hooker and Co., Cincinnati

Railroad Gazette, New York

Rand Drill Co., New York

Reading Hardware Co., New York

Mrs. Sylvanus Reed, Locust, N. J.

Reedy River Manufacturing Co., Greenville, S. C.

John Reid, New York

Otto M. Reimers and Co., New York

Robbins and Appleton, New York

Livingston Roe, New York

Rogers, Brown and Co., New York

Rogers Locomotive Co., Patterson, N. J.

Rump and Cattus, New York

Sale and Co., Yokohama

E. H. Sampson, New York

Charles A. Schieren and Co., New York

J. and W. Seligman and Co., New York

William Sellers and Co., Philadelphia

Augustus D. Shepard, New York

Shewan, Tomes and Co., New York

Sims-Dudley Defence Co., New York

W. and J. Sloane, New York

E. Holden Smith, New York

Smith, Hogg and Gardner, New York

R. B. Smith, New York

Smith and Schipper, New York

Southern Pacific Co., New York

E. G. Spilsbury Engineering Co., New York
Spartan Mills, Spartanburg, S. C.
Theodore Staubli, New York
W. H. Stevens, New York
James Stillman, New York
Samuel Thomas, New York
Henry B. Thompson, Wilmington, Del.
John Thomson Press Co., New York
J. Kennedy Tod, New York
Calvin Tompkins, New York
D. A. Tompkins, Charlotte, N. C.
A. M. Townsend, New York
J. Spencer Turner Co., New York
U. S. Export Assoc., New York
Vacuum Oil Co., Rochester, N. Y.
A. A. Vantine and Co., New York
Verona Tool Works, Pittsburgh
Vesta Mills, Charleston, S. C.
William H. Wallace and Co., New York
Weld and Neville, New York
Western Electric Co., New York

Westinghouse Electric and Manufacturing Co., New York
Thomas R. Wheelock, Boston, Mass.
Wheelwright, Eldredge and Co., New York
Whitney Manufacturing Co., Whitney, S. C.
Charles A. Whittier, New York
Franklin A. Wilcox, New York
E. A. Willard, New York
Willett and Gray, New York
Frederick Wells Williams, New Haven, Conn.
Louis Windmuller, New York
C. R. Winslow and Co., San Francisco
Winter and Smillie, New York
William H. Wisner and Co., New York
Woodward, Baldwin and Co., New York
Yale and Towne Manufacturing Co., New York
Capt. E. L. Zalinski, New York

BIBLIOGRAPHICAL NOTE

Perhaps the best accounts of China's international relations during the nineteenth century are in H. B. Morse, *International Relations of the Chinese Empire* (3 vols., London and New York, 1910–18), and P. H. Clyde, *A History of the Modern and Contemporary Far East; a Survey of Western Contacts with Eastern Asia during the Nineteenth and Twentieth Centuries* (New York, 1937). An excellent detailed treatment of the particular years under investigation in the present volume is P. Joseph, *Foreign Diplomacy in China, 1894–1900, a Study in Political and Economic Relations with China* (London, 1928). Two noteworthy books concerning American policy toward China in the nineteenth century are T. Dennett, *Americans in Eastern Asia; a Critical Study of the Policy of the United States with Regard to China, Japan, and Korea in the 19th Century* (New York, 1922), and F. R. Dulles, *Americans in the Pacific; a Century of Expansion* (Boston and New York, 1932).

Scores of other books and articles have been written on the subject of China's international relations, many of them with particular reference to Sino-American relations. A convenient way to find their titles is through the extensive bibliographies in T. W. Overlach, *Foreign Financial Control in China* (New York, 1919); P. H. Clyde, *International Rivalries in Manchuria* (Columbus, 1926); G. N. Steiger, *China and the Occident, the Origin and Development of the Boxer Movement* (New Haven, 1927); and R. S. McCordock, *British Far Eastern Policy, 1894–1900* (New York, 1931).

The present study is the only one devoted to an investigation of the influence of special business interests upon the adoption of the Open Door Policy. There are only two other books that go beyond the most general observations on this subject, but neither of them deals primarily with the Open Door. Both are definitive on their particular subjects, and both provide excellent starting points for an intensive examination of business and the Open Door. The authors and titles of these two books are J. W. Pratt, *Expansionists of 1898; the Acquisition of Hawaii and the Spanish Islands* (Baltimore, 1936), and A. Vagts, *Deutschland und die Vereinigten Staaten in der Weltpolitik* (2 vols., New York, 1935).

Other writers have limited themselves almost exclusively to an appraisal of the diplomatic factors that had a part in bringing about the Open Door Policy. S. Tomimas, *The Open Door Policy and the Territorial Integrity of China; with Verses in Japanese* (New York, 1919), presents an orderly arrangement of the conventional material but is distinguished chiefly by the pages devoted to Japanese verse. M. J. Bau, *The Open Door Doctrine in Relation to China* (New York, 1923), is uninspired but useful for its concise, comprehensive account of the diplomatic background. E. T. Yen, *The Open Door Policy* (Boston, 1923), is of some use as one of the very few books on the subject. A. L. P. Dennis, *Adventures in American Diplomacy, 1896–1906* (New York, 1928), and A. W. Griswold, *The Far Eastern Policy of the United States* (New York, 1938), although concerned only in part with the Open Door are more penetrating than Yen. Both these volumes put the usual stress upon diplomatic influences and both emphasize the part played by W. W. Rockhill and Alfred Hippisley.

I have found the above-mentioned titles useful mainly for background information. Since no other writer has given particular attention to the influence of business a great part of the present volume is necessarily based on primary material. Of the greatest importance are three sources of information on the American Asiatic Association and its predecessor, the Committee on American Interests in China. Shortly after its formation the association printed a pamphlet entitled *The American Asiatic Association, 1899*. This publication is packed with details regarding the purposes, membership, and early operations of the association. The Minute-Book of the American Asiatic Association, 1898–1919, is a manuscript, much of it in the handwriting of John Foord, which is a most valuable record, although rather cursory, of business conducted at meetings of the executive committee. At an early date the association began to publish a magazine entitled *Asia; Journal of the American Asiatic Association*. Its pages are full of helpful material concerning the association. A fertile field of information regarding both the Asiatic Association and the Committee on American Interests is a New York newspaper, the *Journal of Commerce and Commercial Bulletin*. Its usefulness is not surprising when one recalls that John Foord was an editor. Another reason for consulting the *Journal* is that it furnishes ample evidence of the deep interest in China of the American cotton industry. Invaluable are the Miscellaneous Letters of the Department of State. In this enormous collection there are hundreds of communications to the department, many of them from business concerns, with reference to policy toward China. They furnish insight into the point of view of the many representative writers, and they indicate some of the steps which these men took to influence the government. No account of the Open Door Policy can be complete without careful examination of the Miscellaneous Letters.

No other material is so directly related to the subject of business pressure as that described in the preceding paragraph. But information giving nearly as much insight into the subject is available elsewhere and merits close attention. Other State Department series, notably the Instructions and Despatches, provide illumination. The annual reports of chambers of commerce, boards of trade, and similar commercial organizations are rewarding fields of study; of these the reports of the Chamber of Commerce of the State of New York are particularly relevant to the present book. The various business newspapers and magazines are indispensable. The papers of W. W. Rockhill, John Hay, and William McKinley, although seldom bearing directly on the subject of business pressure, are often revealing. *The Chronicle and Directory for China, Japan, Strait Settlements, Indo-China, the Philippines, etc., for the Year 1900* (Hongkong, 1900), is occasionally helpful, as are the Foreign Office records in the Public Records Office, London.

I have made general use of the above-mentioned titles throughout the book as a whole. Certain material, on the other hand, I have used only with reference to the subject matter of particular chapters.

Business periodicals and the reports of commercial organizations are revealing as to the widespread fear in the 1890's that the home market was saturated and that the country was endangered by a rapidly growing surplus. Among the many articles and books dealing with the bogey of the surplus the following are some of the most significant: A. T. Mahan, *Lessons of the War with Spain* (Boston, 1899); F. Emory, "Our Commercial Expansion," *Munsey's Magazine, 22* (1900), 538–544, is worth reading because Emory was in 1899 and 1900 chief of the Bureau of Foreign and Domestic Commerce; Brooks Adams, *America's Economic Supremacy* (New York, 1900); Whitelaw Reid, *Problems of Expansion, as Considered in Papers and Addresses* (New York, 1900). The books by Reid and Mahan indicate the vigorous policy advocated by two leaders of the Large Policy.

As regards the American commercial invasion of Europe and the American reaction to rumors of concerted European policy, I have found several works of particular help. A. D. Noyes, *Forty Years of American Finance* (New York and London, 1898), has an account of the Goluchowski incident. Brooks Adams, "Reciprocity or the Alternative," *The Atlantic Monthly, 88* (1901), 145–155, considers both the American commercial advance and the reaction of Europe. An anonymous article, "Two Presidents and the Limits of American Supremacy," *Fortnightly Review, 76* (1901), 555–570, is worth attention as an instance of refusal to became alarmed over the American invasion. S. Brooks, "Europe and America," *The Atlantic Monthly, 88* (1901), 577–588, shows how seriously many Americans regarded the possibility of an European combination. On the other hand, an editorial entitled "Europe and the 'American Peril,'" *The Nation, 73* (1901), 5–6, takes a less alarmist point of view. C. Furness, "The Old World and the American 'Invasion,'" *Pall Mall Magazine, 26* (1902), 362–368, views the invasion rather calmly from Great Britain, while M. Prager, "Die Amerikanische Gefahr," *Volkswirthschaftliche Zeitfragen* (Berlin, 1902), presents a more agitated German reaction. J. H. Clapham, *An Economic History of Modern Britain, Machines and National Rivalries (1887–1914), with an Epilogue (1914–1929)* (3 vols., Cambridge, 1926–38), has an excellent analysis of American competition.

The most penetrating study of the Large Policy is J. W. Pratt, *Expan-*

sionists of 1898; the Acquisition of Hawaii and the Spanish Islands (Baltimore, 1936).

The best sources of material on the vision of the potential Chinese market are business periodicals, business newspapers, and reports of various commercial organizations. But other sources are well worth attention. G. N. Curzon, *Problems of the Far East* (Westminister, 1896), shows the appeal which the potential market had for a prominent Englishman. C. Cary, "China's Complications and American Trade," *The Forum, 25* (1898), 35–45, and *China's Present and Prospective Railways* (New York, 1899), express the convictions of an influential figure in the origins of the Open Door Policy. C. Denby, Jr., "America's Opportunity in Asia," *The North American Review, 166* (1898), 32–39, is significant partly because the son of the minister to China was himself a zealous proponent of a strong American policy in the Far East. Similarly, J. Barrett, "The Paramount Power of the Pacific," *The North American Review, 169* (1899), 165–179, and "America's Duty in China," *The North American Review, 171* (1900), 145–157, require notice as expressions of a man who resigned from the diplomatic service in order to campaign for American intervention. in China. Several other articles by Barrett exist in various periodicals but the above two are the most pertinent. A. T. Mahan, *The Problems of Asia and Its Effect upon International Policies* (Boston, 1900), gives occasional illumination. C. A. Conant, *The United States in the Orient, the Nature of the Economic Problem* (Boston and New York, 1900), argues for recognition of an American stake in China. W. W. Rockhill, "The United States and the Future of China," *The Forum, 29* (1900), 324–331, is unimportant except as the utterance of an influential man. A. J. Beveridge, *The Russian Advance* (New York and London, 1903), pays considerable deference to the idea of a potential market.

Statistical and other information on American trade with China is readily available in United States government publications. A book which must be consulted by any student of the period is F. H. Hitchcock, *Our Trade with Japan, China, and Hongkong, 1889–1899* (Washington, 1900). Three books by C. F. Remer are helpful for the general background. They are *The Foreign Trade of China* (Shanghai, 1926); *American Investments in China* (Honolulu 1929); and *Foreign Investments in China* (New York, 1933). Ping-yin Ho, *The Foreign Trade of China* (Shanghai, 1935), has some merit; but a much more helpful book because of its analysis of specific American products exported to China is Shu-lun Pan, *The Trade of the United States with China* (New York, 1924).

D. A. Tompkins, *National Expansion* (Charlotte, 1899), gives the views of a leader of southern cotton interests. Nos. 5–8 of the issue for 1899–1900 of a publication of the United States Government, *Monthly Summary of Commerce and Finance of the United States,* contain a detailed treatment of American cotton exports. R. M. Odell, *Cotton Goods in China* (Washington, 1916), is informative although for the most part with reference to the years after 1900. M. T. Copeland, *The Cotton-Manufacturing Industry in the United States* (Cambridge, 1912), has an extensive and helpful bibliography.

Considerable material on the American-China Development Company is stored in the files of the State Department. W. B. Parsons, *An American Engineer in China* (New York, 1900), a book written by the Development Company's chief engineer, is disappointingly barren of pertinent material. Good general accounts not limited to the Development Company are P. H. Kent, *Railway Enterprise in China* (London, 1907), and A. J. Barry, "Railway Development in China," *Journal of the Royal Society of Arts, 57* (1909), 541–558. M. C. Hsu, *Railroad Problems in China* (New York, 1915), gives the general picture but is not particularly relevant to an investigation of special business interests.

INDEX

AFRICA, 11

American Asiatic Association, 16, 51,
59, 61, 66; and Boxers, 68–71; and
commercial commission, 64–65; influence, 44, 46, 52, 53, 56–58, 73–74;
and International Settlement, 48–49;
and *Journal of Commerce*, 44; July
circular, reaction to, 73–74; membership, 42–43, Appendix; purposes, 42;
and San Mun Bay, 50, 53; September
notes, reaction to, 56–59

American Association of China, 48, 57;
and Boxers, 68–69; consular service
reform, 62; establishment, 42

American-China Development Company, 28, 29, 42, 43, 51, 57, 66, 72; and
Boxers, 67, 70–71; and China, 22–23,
26; contracts, 39, 60–61, 72–73; and
July circular, 72; membership, 21–22;
and Russia, 27; and September notes,
56

American Peril, 5

American Sugar Refineries Company,
22

*Asia; Journal of the American Asiatic
Association*, 42, 44

Austria-Hungary, 6, 7, 8

BAKER, GEORGE F., 22

Baldwin Locomotive Works, 70

Balfour, Arthur, 45

Baltimore Chamber of Commerce,
34

Barings, the, 39

Barrett, John, 52, 60, 61, 63, 70; China,
policy advocated toward, 43–44; influence, 58; purpose, statement of, 43
n. 22

Barry, Sir John W. B., 39

Bash, A. W., 26–29, 71

Beresford, Lord Charles, 50, 51

Bethlehem Iron Company, 30

Beveridge, A. J., 4, 5

Bliss, C. N., 36, 61

Bliss, Fabyan and Company, 36, 47

Bonsor, Cosmo, 39

Boston: Board of Trade, 63; Chamber
of Commerce, 12, 34, 35–36, 63

Boxers, 46, 65, 67–73

Bradstreet's, 2, 12, 14

Brewster, S. D., 30, 42; American Asiatic Association, appraisal of, 73–74

Brice, Calvin S., 21, 43

British and China Association, 60, 73;
and American-China Development
Company, 39–40

British China Association, 35, 41, 48

Businessmen, 33, 51, 60; and China, 10–
18, 19–24, 59, 61, 71; and foreign
policy, 12–13; and the government, 66,
71; Great Britain, opinion of, 33, 51,
52, 60; July circular, reaction to, 71–
74; overproduction, fear of, 1–9; September notes, reaction to, 56–57, 59–
66

CABLE, PACIFIC, 17, 60

Canada Club, 8

Canal, 13–14, 17, 60

Carnegie Steel Company, 22

Cary and Whitridge, 40

Cary, Clarence, 22, 28, 51, 54, 60, 61, 69;
and Boxers, 69–71; and commercial
commission, 64; influence, 42, 43;
Sherman, opinion of, 30

Central Trust Company of New York,
22

Chamberlain, Joseph, 8, 15, 45

Chicago Board of Trade, 12, 63

Chicago Inter Ocean, 68

China: as market, 8, 9, 19–20; and Monroe Doctrine, 13; threats to, 15, 25,
45–52; wars of, 15, 67

China and Japan Trading Company, 36

Cleveland: Board of Trade, 63; Chamber of Commerce, 3, 34, 62

Colonial Conference, 8

Commercial and Financial Chronicle, 6

Commercial commission, 38, 68; de-
bated, 63–66

Committee on American Interests in
China, 30, 37, 38, 41; petition of, 34–
35

Conant, Charles A., 26, 53
Conger, Edwin, 47, 48, 49, 57
Connecticut State Board of Trade, 1, 16
Consular service reform, 3, 61–62
Cosmos Club, 64
Coster, Charles, 22
Cotton, raw, 19 n. 1
Cotton textile industry, 20, 21, 50, 72; and Boxers, 68; and canal, 14; and China, 19, 20, 21, 47, 59, 60, 66; July circular, reaction to, 72; September notes, reaction to, 56; see also New England Cotton Manufacturers' Association; Southern Cotton Spinners' Association
Croydon Chamber of Commerce, 8

Dana, Paul, 49
Davis, C. K., 30
Day, W. R., 46; and American-China Development Company, 39–40; and commercial commission, 38, 63
Deering, Milliken and Company, 30, 47, 70
Denby, Charles, 25, 33–34, 43; and American-China Development Company, 26–29
Denby, Charles, Jr., 39, 43 n. 22
Dewey, Admiral, 15, 40
Diamond Match Company, 43
Dingley, Nelson, 30
Dingley Tariff Act, 7

Equitable Life Assurance Society of the United States, 43, 70
Europe, commercial union of, 5–8; see also Goluchowski

Fearon, Daniel and Company, 58, 70
Fearon, J. S., 58, 64
First National Bank of New York, 22
Flour, 23
Foord, John, 26, 30, 36, 41, 44, 50, 54, 69; and Boxers, 70; and commercial commission, 64–65; influence, 42, 43
France, 15, 21, 25, 32, 48, 55
Frazar, Everett, 30, 42, 48 n. 20, 51, 54, 56, 57, 61, 65, 68, 69
Frazar and Company, 30, 70
Frye, Senator W. P., 17, 49, 65
Fukien, 32

Gallinger-Hepburn bill, 63–65
General Electric Company, 43
Germany, 7, 8, 15, 55; and Kiaochao, 25, 37; and Shantung, 32, 49, 65
Gibbs, Anthony and Company, 39
Goluchowski, Count, 6, 7, 8, 15
Great Britain, 5, 14, 15, 20, 32, 33, 55; and imperial preference, 8; and Open Door, 32, 52
Great Northern Railroad Company, 43
Guaranty Trust Company, 43, 70

Hainan, 25, 32
Hambro interests, 39
Hanna, Mark, 15, 65
Harriman, E. H., 22
Hawaii, 16, 17
Hay, John, 46, 54, 56, 57, 59, 60, 61, 62, 65, 69, 70, 71, 73; China, policy toward, 47–50
Hegeman, G. R., 22
Hepburn, Representative. See Gallinger-Hepburn bill
Hill, D. J., 70
Hippisley, Alfred, 53, 54, 72
Hitchcock, Ambassador, 37
Hoar, Senator G. F., 16
Hongkong and Shanghai Bank, 32, 39
Hongkong Chamber of Commerce, 61

Imperialism, 15
India, 20
International Commercial Congress, 61
International Settlement, 48
Iron Age, 2, 12
Iron and steel, exports of, 23–24, 24 n. 23
Italy, 55; see also San Mun Bay

Japan, 10, 32, 55
Jardine, Matheson and Company, 39
Jesup, Morris K., 43
Journal of Commerce and Commercial Bulletin, 2, 6, 7, 12, 15, 38, 42, 44, 46, 49, 57; and Boxers, 68; China, attitude toward, 26; influence, 53; and Sherman, 30
July circular, Introduction, 67–74; text, 71

Kerosene, 23
Kiaochao, 25, 37
Kowloon, 33
Kuhn, Loeb and Company, 22
Kwanchow-wan, 32

Large Policy, 4, 15, 26
Liaotung Peninsula, 33
Literary Digest, 67
Lodge, Henry Cabot, 4–5, 65
London Chamber of Commerce, 61
Low, Seth, 43

McGee, James, 30
McKinley, William, 1, 40, 52, 65, 68, 70, 71; and Open Door Policy, 54–55, 57; annual message for 1898, 46, for 1899, 4
McLaurin, Senator, 65
Madagascar, 21
Mahan, A. T., 4
Manhattan Trust Company, 22
Manila Bay, battle of, 15, 40
Manufacturers' Association of Illinois, 2
Manufacturers' Association of Philadelphia, 62
Markets, struggle for, 4
Maryland Steel Company, 43
Mercantile Trust Company, 43
Merchants' Association of New York, 3
Merchants' Exchange of St. Louis, 15
Metropolitan Life Insurance Company, 22
Monroe Doctrine, 13
Moreing, C. A., 11
Morgan, J. P. and Company, 22
Morton, Levi P., 21
Mutual Life Insurance Company of New York, 43

National Association of Manufacturers, 2, 12, 64, 66; and Shanghai warehouse, 62–63
National Board of Trade, 59, 63
National Business League of Chicago, 62
National City Bank, 22
New England Cotton Manufacturers' Association, 60

New England Shoe and Leather Association, 36
New Orleans Board of Trade, 14
Newport News Shipbuilding and Dry Dock Company, 43
New York Board of Trade and Transportation, 63
New York Central and Hudson River Railroad Company, 43
New York Chamber of Commerce, 3, 51, 52, 63; and consular service reform, 62; and Hay, 47, 48; resolutions of, 34–35, 38, 62
New York Times, 7
North American Review, 53

Olcott, F. P., 21
Olney, Richard, 27, 28
Open Door Policy, Introduction, 1, 9, 21, 24, 41, 58, 61, 62, 71, 72, 74
Oukhtomsky, Prince Esper, 53
Overproduction. *See* Surplus

Pacific Cable Company of New York, 43
Parsons, Gen. W. B., 39, 60–61, 70
Peirce, H. H. D., 47
Pepperell Manufacturing Company, 43, 47
Philadelphia: Board of Trade, 34, 35, 63; Commercial Museum, 3, 61, 70
Philadelphia Inquirer, 17
Philadelphia Press, 30, 34, 46
Philippine Islands, 16, 45; annexation of, 15–16, 17, 41; and Open Door Policy, 41, 60
Pillsbury-Washburn Flour Company, 28
Platt, Thomas C., 21
Port Arthur. *See* Russia
Proctor, John R., 13

Ritchie, Charles T., 8
Rockefeller interests, 22
Rockhill, W. W., 43, 55, 62, 64, 70, 72; and American Asiatic Association, 54
Rogers Locomotive Company, 70
Roosevelt, Theodore, 4
Rothschild interests, 39
Russia, 7, 8, 15, 53, 55; and Boxers, 69, 70; and North China and Manchuria,

Russia (*continued*)
  20, 21, 27, 47, 52; and Port Arthur, 25, 32, 33, 37

St. Louis Board of Trade, 63
San Francisco: Chamber of Commerce, 12, 16, 17, 34, 35; Manufacturers' and Producers' Association, 16; Merchants' Association, 16
San Mun Bay, 49–50, 51, 53
Sassoon interests, 39
Schiff, Jacob H., 22
Schurman, J. G., 55
Scott-Mouravieff convention, 51–52
Search, Theodore C., 64
Seattle Chamber of Commerce, 16, 34
September notes, Introduction, 54, 56, 59, 61, 65, 66, 68, 70; text, 55
Shanghai: Chamber of Commerce, 61, 62; concession in, 48; warehouse, 62–63
Shantung Province, 25, 32, 49, 65
Sherman, John, 38, 46, 53, 72; character, 28–29; Denby, rebukes, 29; and New York Chamber of Commerce, 37; *Philadelphia Press,* interview with, 30
Sino-Japanese War, 15
South America, 8, 9
South Carolina, 20, 60
Southern Cotton Spinners' Association, 17, 60, 64
Spain, war with, 4, 15, 38–44
Standard Oil Company, 30
Stillman, James, 22
Surplus, 1–12
Sutherland, Sir Thomas, 39

Talienwan, 33, 53
Thielmann, Baron von, 7
Times Herald, Chicago, 16
Times Picayune, New Orleans, 13
Tongking, 32
Tower, Ambassador, 6–7, 8
Trade-Review, Houston, 14
Trading houses, 24
Transcript, Boston, 46
Trans-Mississippi Commercial Congress, 63
Trans-Siberian Railway, 7, 26

Union Pacific Railway, 22
United States: and China, Introduction, 71, exports to, 9, 10–11, 17–18; and foreign investments, 22; foreign trade, trend of, 1–2
United States Export Association, 64, 70
United States Investor, 2, 13, 45–46

Wanghia, treaty of, 10
Washburn, W. D., 28, 43
Washington, George, 13
Waterbury, John I., 22
Weihaiwei, 33
Whang Poo River, 62
White, Ambassador, 8, 37
Wilson, W. P., 70
Wu Ting Fang, 61, 72

Yellow Peril, 5

Zalinski, E. L., 30